"Born dead is not exactly the best start to life—but that is how David's story begins. Don't miss one riveting page."

—Franklin Graham, president, Billy Graham Evangelistic Association

"Sometimes the challenges a person with a disability experiences are not what you'd expect. David Ring shares how family and friendship helped shape his indomitable spirit, strong character, and remarkable zeal for life. Best of all, we learn how God used his limitations to develop a much-beloved message of grace and hope that would expand beyond his wildest dreams."

—Joni Eareckson Tada, Joni and Friends International Disability Center

"Nothing forces us to grow in every area of life like adversity. And I don't know anyone who's become more successful by overcoming more challenges than David Ring."

—Dave Ramsey, *New York Times* bestselling author and nationally syndicated radio show host

"Very few people can speak to adversity and overcoming obstacles with greater authority than David."

—from the foreword by Mike Huckabee

"In the following pages you will begin to realize that living is more than being healthy, happy, or normal. You will come to understand that living can include struggle and pain. Living doesn't necessarily belong to those with strong bodies as much as it does to those with transformed spirits that are made invincible. I'm so excited for you to read this story about a boy born dead, who discovered what it means to truly live. I'm eager for you to have the same opportunity that I enjoyed: to experience David up close and to discover for yourself that the closer you get, the more alive he is!"

—Danny deArmas, senior associate pastor, First Baptist Orlando

THE BOY BORN DEAD

A Story of Friendship, Courage, and Triumph

DAVID RING
with JOHN DRIVER
and DAVID WIDEMAN

a division of Baker Publishing Group
Grand Rapids, Michigan

Published by Baker Books
a division of Baker Publishing Group
P.O. Box 6287, Grand Rapids, MI 49516-6287
www.bakerbooks.com

Paperback edition published 2016
ISBN 978-0-8010-1945-6

Printed in the United States of America

Library of Congress Cataloging-in-Publication Data has cataloged the previous edition as follows:
Ring, David 1953–
The boy born dead: a story of friendship, courage, and triumph / David Ring, with John Driver and David Wideman.
pages cm
ISBN 978-0-8010-1730-8 (cloth)
1. Ring, David, 1953– . Christian biography—Missouri—Liberty. 3. Cerebral palsied—Missouri—Liberty—Biography. I. Wideman, David. II. Driver, John, 1978– III. Title.
BR1725.R574A3 2015
269′.2092—dc23 2015010416

Although this is a work of nonfiction, certain events have been altered or fictionalized for the sake of condensing the factual events into narrative form. Some of the names and details of people have been changed to protect the privacy of those involved.

The author is represented by the literary agency of Wolgemuth & Associates, Inc.

16 17 18 19 20 21 22 7 6 5 4 3 2 1

In keeping with biblical principles of creation stewardship, Baker Publishing Group advocates the responsible use of our natural resources. As a member of the Green Press Initiative, our company uses recycled paper when possible. The text paper of this book is composed in part of post-consumer waste.

Foreword

Life isn't fair. It is a phrase we begin to hear sometime in our early childhood. Well, hopefully we hear it, because regardless of whether or not we do, it is an inescapable truth. Storms come. Dishes break. People face hardship. Whether we avoid thinking about it or declare it to be the greatest injustice, fairness is simply not a feature of the world we currently live in.

I suppose this reality is the truest essence of any story: what we do with the unfair things in life.

If you think about it, that is also the essence of the story of our own nation, even from its earliest toddlerhood. The colonial patriots were, in fact, rebels against something unfair and unjust. Sharing a common birthplace and a common language, they refused to share a common king with their cousins across the ocean. They became courageously uncommon in the midst of cultural commonalities, not content to let the unfairness of taxation or representation become a very blunt period at the end of a very brief sentence.

Because of how they faced their particular unfairness, they had a story to tell.

The story that follows is also a rebel's tale. And much like the diversity of stories and lore that swirl about our nation's founders and the events surrounding their fight against the unfairness, the essential heart of this narrative and its details are steeped in truth. That is what makes it more than just a story. That is what makes it alive.

I can most certainly promise you that the words to follow are more than you probably think they are, and vastly so. I know this to be true because it was a significantly more compelling narrative than I had anticipated, and I've known David Ring since the 1970s, when I first heard him share his incredible testimony on television. I later met him on several occasions, during various conferences and events. It was early on in our friendship that I learned what you will soon learn as well: very few people can speak to adversity and overcoming obstacles with greater authority than David can. I, like millions of others around the globe, have never heard him speak without being blown away by the power of his message and the clarity of his life story.

But as this book will prove, there is so much more to the story than I thought I knew.

To listen to David Ring speak is one thing—and that thing itself should not be quickly passed by. David has cerebral palsy and his delivery of words can, at first, be painful both in the delivery and the listening. Yet I have never seen a person in his hearing who does not quickly move from endurance to emotion to energy. Why? Because they are forced to face unfairness in a way they never have before—and witness firsthand a courageous mutiny from one of its most ravaged victims. They see that David Ring refuses to remain a victim despite all the immensely valid reasons he has to do so.

Yet despite this most amazing interaction that occurs between stuttering speaker and unsuspecting listener, the full scope of David's story has never been told . . . until now.

David Ring and his coauthors have now removed the obstacles of time and limitation to let us walk through his amazing story, focusing on his teen years in the 1960s in the small town of Liberty, Missouri. With a bit of color and minor fictionalized characters added to certain parts of the narrative to help it move along, this particular story becomes unbelievably believable. It is unbelievable because the unfairness is so fierce, yet the authentic grace David experiences in God and in relationships with the people God placed into his life is even fiercer. It is believable because the nuts and bolts of the story are true.

This story is told from the perspective of David Wideman, a young man who befriended a very different David Ring when he moved to Liberty to finish high school after the death of his mother. The riveting story of how they became and still remain friends reminds us all of a familiar truth often lost in its own repetition: God's grace has no boundaries or limits. I implore you not to look past it, for it remains the catalyst for rebels everywhere who desire to overcome unfairness. Trust me, if anyone is feeling sorry for themselves, feeling that "life isn't fair," this book will be a wake-up call and a humbling experience.

Because of how David and his friends faced their particular unfairness, there is a story to tell.

Somewhere in our own history, someone felt a divine inclination to rebel against unfairness. To not let circumstances eclipse a grace that promised to be greater still. In that moment, a revolution began that led to something infinitely more grandiose than the patriots ever dreamed. David Ring is also a rebel, not against grace but rather for it. And as you read his story, you will sense a revolution.

Mike Huckabee

This is David Ring's story, written from the perspective of his friend David Wideman.

1

It must have played a thousand times in the theater of my mind, probably fueled by too many old western flicks on late-night television.

The bank teller's hands thrust into the air. The outlaw's words, muffled by the faded red kerchief covering his mouth. "Just fill the bag, old-timer, and nobody gets hurt!"

With no more than a furtive glance at the wild eyes of the desperado, the teller begins to stuff bills into the sack. He knows it's a moment he'll never forget, a half-face to haunt his dreams through the rest of his old age. The light gleams off the Colt Army Model 1860 revolver in the bandit's hand.

I have the outlaw's backstory memorized. He took that gun from the bloody corpse of A.V. E. Johnson, Union major, during the Centralia Massacre of the "late unpleasantness" also known as the Civil War. He rode with Confederate guerrillas, a band of thugs really, as they brought terror to the countryside.

In my imaginary western, the gang rides away with the loot. The Clay County Savings Association has been bled all but dry, and the robbers have pulled off the first daylight armed bank robbery in the United States during peacetime.

I grew up with the tale. Everybody in Liberty, Missouri, did. These outlaws—the James brothers, Frank and Jesse—have a certain place in American lore, but in Liberty they're bigger than life. Sooner or later, you hear the stories, you watch a film or two, and then you want the true narrative.

The history books tell you that the James brothers were actually the sons of a preacher, one Robert S. James. Along with launching two bloodthirsty offspring, he also helped launch a fine institution of learning, William Jewell College—a mixed legacy to be sure. The bank and the school stood in the same town, looting and learning brought together. The good reverend himself moved on, heading west with a vision of ministering to those caught up in the fever of the Gold Rush. And there he died of some other fever entirely.

Liberty had not grown to become another Montgomery or Memphis. It was a quieter town, located about twenty miles outside of Kansas City, near the geographical center of the continental United States.

The heart of the town rested upon three hilltops. The most westward hill was home to Liberty High School. Each year, the homecoming parade would start at the high school and lead down through a valley and back up to the center-most hilltop. The roadside would be littered with remnants of the fun. Crinkled tissue paper that had come unglued from the homecoming floats. Single flower petals unlatched from the blooms that donned the many corsages and boutonnieres of the young couples. That center hill was topped by the town square, which included the courthouse and other old buildings. It was on the steps of the courthouse that the homecoming queen would be announced.

The third and easternmost hill contained the campus of William Jewell College. During the Civil War, the Union army took over some of the buildings, using them as their hospitals and burying their dead on campus. I know it sounds morbid, but I always loved the idea that dead men were buried somewhere under that hill. No one could see them, but they were there. Reminders that blood and history and the hearts of our forefathers were never far away. They may have been unseen, but they were still a part of us, even if only six feet beneath our daily walk.

By the time I was a teenager, Liberty was a prototypical Midwestern American town. We spent summer days partaking of the soda fountain, a surefire relief from the blistering heat. Soda was the antidote for sweat, even though it made us thirstier. It was one of those childhood mysteries that rocked the boat of the laws of the universe and never apologized for doing so. We had our own cosmos, and among those stars it was a fact that sugar, syrup, and bubbly water produced a certain heavenly nectar.

But the sweetest things were those we took for granted.

Things like childhood. Long summer days exploring old Mr. Maxwell's woods. Throwing rocks at the window shutters of the abandoned farmhouse out on Rodes Street—a funny name for a street, I always thought. They could have called it Rodes Road, but duller heads prevailed.

That house was completely dilapidated. My dad told me that it had once belonged to an old man who had ridden with Teddy Roosevelt and the Rough Riders down in Texas. He bought the land and built the house with his bare hands. But he never married. Too cantankerous to live with. Stubborn and loud. He would often discharge his rifle at lightning bugs—from his front porch. I'm not sure he ever hit one, but he was the kind of guy you'd never visit unannounced. Unless you were driving a tank.

When he died, no one came forward as his next of kin, so the land and house just sat empty for years. Our game was to see who could hit the shutters the most times in a row without missing. Hitting the old wood siding meant no points. But if you ever heard glass break, you automatically won because most of the glass had been gone for years—evidence of all the young adventurers who had thrown rocks before us.

Nights were best spent across the street at the ice cream parlor. It was the perfect destination to impress a girl with a cherry-topped milkshake with two straws. Down the street was Fisher's Flower Shop, where I worked my first job. Walk a little farther and there was Frederick's Hardware Store, which had been open for more than fifty years. Frederick's had ladders mounted along racks, a bit like library ladders, allowing customers to climb the shelves and find whatever screw, nut, or bolt they needed on any shelf of any height.

Beside the old spring, a mill had been built before the War Between the States. The train tracks wound their way in and about the mill, eventually meandering into town. Some years later, when the mill was torn down, rats escaped the old building and entered the sewer system. They decided to make unexpected appearances by the hundreds in the homes of local residents. In Liberty, not even the rats liked change.

The Missouri River anchored the southern border of the city, separating it from the town of Independence on its way toward a meeting with the mighty Mississippi River in St. Louis. My friends and I used to say that the only difference between liberty and independence was a river. The Missouri was known as the watery highway for old steamships in the 1850s, so much so that more than two hundred and fifty of these antique vessels still lie entombed on the cold floor of the riverbed—irresistible sirens beckoning treasure hunters aching for lost gold and gamblers' spoils.

That was Liberty in 1969, when this story began for me. Some people called it the heartland. Me? I'd say more like the eye of the hurricane. While storms raged from the blood-stained streets of America's urban hotbeds to the steamy jungles of Vietnam, we were staying pretty safe and dry here in the center.

I do not remember caring about the color of anyone's skin, nor did anyone seem to care about mine. Even so, I suppose I cared enough to remember that my class had a couple hundred students in it but only about five of them were black. We knew that we had our differences, but I guess we just didn't care as much about those differences as others seemed to in other parts of the country. Around here, there were no separate water fountains marked "white" or "colored." No signs posted prohibiting anyone from doing anything because of race. For a town in the 1960s, we were actually pretty progressive when it came to that kind of stuff.

I did not recognize it as such at the time, but that teenage version of me thought nothing could ever get to us in Liberty. I subconsciously believed our currents would continue to flow and trickle as they always had. What reason did they have to change?

As I would soon discover, the reason was coming. He was limping his way to catch a school bus on a September day in 1969, walking there by himself from Lewis Street, just a few blocks from the church.

Few would have taken much notice of the awkward, shambling figure. He couldn't have been made in any image more different from the rugged western outlaw Jesse James. Yet this figure, like that one, would have a brother in arms. If those were the James brothers, we were the Davids, because we shared a first name. And we had our own adventures, though guns and banks were not involved.

If Jesse James became known across the world for what he stole, David Ring has become famous for what he gave. If Jesse brought blood, terror, and death, my Liberty brother has offered something as close to the opposite as could be imagined. If the old outlaw represented the illusion of power, then my good friend has represented the power of weakness.

David Ring didn't have the bravado that comes to those with a gun and a mask. His bravery shone through in the obstacles he overcame. And bearing witness to this changed my concept of normal as well. I'm far from alone in those changes. People across the world, many who have never even met him personally, are different people because of what he has given them.

But I have had the good fortune to know him. I was there for this story. And if there are particular scenes here that I may not have personally witnessed, I have rendered them to the best of my ability through my knowledge of the people, their own accounts, and my imagination of how those scenes transpired.

What follows is a story like none you've ever heard.

2

September 1969

"What is wrong with him? Is he some kind of retard or something?"

Those were the first words I ever heard spoken about him. From the moment I heard them, they affected me. He affected me. I'm not sure why or how. Some themes in our lives we choose, but some choose us. Like happening upon a sunset or catching poison ivy.

For some reason, those words seemed to seek me out in an unexpected way. As if I was destined to hear them. Destined to see the world differently than I had ever seen it before.

It was fall. A season defined by the leaves. The bright oranges and deep reds outlining each street had the artistry of a painter mad with creativity.

Some of the leaves had already lost their battle with the paintbrush, giving up their colors to blandness and crackling.

They were beginning to accent the streets, yards, and sidewalks, though not yet enough to pile and jump into after an afternoon of raking. Just enough to let someone know you were coming.

I never heard the leaves snap when he walked up to the bus stop, which was odd since I could hear my own footsteps. Everyone else crunched and crackled through the leaves. Everyone but him. It was as if he just appeared. When he arrived in our town on that brisk autumn morning, a certain sense of color arrived with him and it immediately began to seep through the cracks of my black and white world.

Dad usually dropped me off at school in his car, but that morning was different. He got a last-second call from someone in trouble who needed to talk. When I asked him who it was, he gave me that familiar look. Ministerial confidentiality and whatnot. So I rode with him to church with the intention of catching the bus at the stop just a few streets down from there, on Prairie. At the time it just seemed like another abnormal normality of being a minister's kid. Just something that happened by chance.

I wasn't supposed to be there, but I was.

The words were spoken just loud enough that everyone at the bus stop could hear them, even him. They came from the mouth of Amy Kline—one of the prettiest and most popular girls in our class. A cheerleader in every way imaginable, all the way to her peppy marrow. She must have come out of her mother's womb with pompoms and that distinctive cheerleader bark that opens up every word to sound like the long vowel sound of the letter *A*. Reeaaady? Okaaay!

"He looks retarded!"

Amy said it in that stage whisper everyone in the audience can hear, and flipped her dirty blonde hair out of her face to catch a better peripheral view of the three other cheerleaders orbiting her gravitational pull. Right on cue, the trio giggled in perfect unison.

I had no time to focus on whatever girl games they were playing. I had more pressing matters on my mind. My gaze was slyly aimed down the sidewalk in the opposite direction—in just that certain way to keep anyone from suspecting I was gazing. For that was the sidewalk lucky enough to be graced by the flawless feet of one Summer Havenstead.

The perfect name for the perfect girl.

Summer Heaven-sent we called her, among ourselves. She lived just a few miles from me but seemed to be from a different planet, one where cosmic beauties were born and transported by spaceship to earth to torture teenage boys. I was her most-tortured victim, though I doubt she ever knew it.

It was not because I was unpopular—to be honest, quite the opposite was true. I was the president of just about every club open to a junior's leadership. And that was where the rub occurred. She was eighteen and a senior and I was neither. In our world, that was a gulf as wide as our river. But there was no law against enjoying the view.

I was no slave of fashion, but I became a student of one particular trend: skintight blue jeans. I studied them enough to earn a graduate degree. I theorized that every morning, Summer floated out of her bed amid leftover moonbeams and lavender vapors, levitating into a special chamber where each majestic stitch of denim was painstakingly lathered onto her perfect body like oiled colors on a Da Vinci masterpiece. No number of buttons or rivets could fully contain such beauty—they merely became decorative accents to her perfection.

She was Los Angeles—an angel above and beyond the rest of us. I was Liberty—and two years too late to her party. We stood only a few feet from each other, but we were worlds apart. Yet the good thing about being sixteen is that no matter how deep the heart bottoms out, it quickly acquires new distractions for comfort. It could be another crush, or it could be something altogether unrelated. Even inanimate. A track meet. An old knife found in your dad's toolbox. In this particular case, the distraction was not a welcome one.

"Hey, David. Are you riding our bus today?" The words broke my trance and, unfortunately, they came from the same chatty Amy Kline who had been whispering before. I was no stranger to Amy. I sat near her and a group of her cronies in English Lit. Their whispering banter was the constant and slightly annoying backdrop to the Shakespeare we were supposed to be studying. *Et tu*, Amy?

I never liked to admit it, but I'm pretty sure Amy had a small crush on me. She wasn't a bad person—fairly easy on the eyes too. Even so, I wasn't very interested at the time. She was a little too talkative for my taste, but most of all, she simply wasn't Summer Havenstead.

"Hey, Amy," I replied. "Yeah, Dad had an appointment at the church. Just hitching a ride."

I replied with little emotion. My mind was still "Summering" elsewhere. But Amy would not be deterred by my dull tone. "So did you study for the English quiz today?"

Her tone was upbeat and hopeful. Not so much about the quiz, but more so about the fact we were having a conversation.

"Eh, a little. I'm not that worried about it."

"Of course you're not," she drawled, really working the flirtatious engines. "You always make perfect grades, Mr. Straight-A Student."

I looked down and shifted my feet a bit. "Yeah, well, I guess I keep getting lucky."

"Oh David! Quit acting modest." She grinned at me. I smiled back, but I knew my smile wasn't the best in my arsenal.

Her grin faded as a little sincerity broke through. "Well, if you ask me, I think we shouldn't have to take all these stupid quizzes anyway." I had already lost interest in the conversation, but she was laboring to extend it.

Then she leaned in close and cupped her hand over my ear to whisper—a key flirtation move, letting her lips lightly brush my ear. "Have you seen the new kid? I think he's retarded or something."

"Amy!" giggled another cheerleader. "You are horrible! He's going to hear you!"

Really? I thought to myself. *As if we couldn't all hear her.* Casually, so as to be discreet, I turned to see whom she was talking about.

Walking toward us was a teenage boy, about my age. I couldn't put my finger on it, but something just wasn't right about him. I mean, he looked kind of normal, I guess. About my height. Definitely skinnier than me, which was a pretty big deal. It made me feel confident that if push came to shove in a backyard game of football, I could probably tackle him pretty easily. It was one of the standard evaluation procedures of adolescent boys: the "tackleability" meter—and this kid bottomed out the scale.

Brown hair. Very fair skin. Blue eyes, not that you could see them at all. He was hunched over so far that he looked like a question mark missing the lower dot. I wasn't sure if he had heard Amy's whispers. If he had, he was not reacting at all. Maybe he didn't understand what she'd said. Maybe he really was retarded.

"What's the matter? Retard got your tongue?"

This time it wasn't Amy. It was Billy Taylor, a senior on the baseball team who had more muscles than brains. I theorized that he had taken a few too many baseballs to the head during batting practice. Others standing at the bus stop chuckled to themselves, but I saw Amy flinch. Billy had taken it a little further than she intended.

The new kid did not acknowledge Billy at all. He just kept walking—if you could call it that. His approach to the bus stop was painfully slow, seemingly both for him and for everyone watching. It was as if he were dragging his own body against its will, towing the weight of the world behind it.

I couldn't tell that anything was actually wrong with his arms or legs, just that they didn't want to cooperate. Their resistance had obviously taken its toll. The new kid looked like a person beaten down in every way. It's hard to put your finger on exactly what makes a human being appear hollow, but whatever it is, he had the worst case of it I had ever seen.

At first, I assumed it was a result of a physical disability. That made sense on the surface, but something about him told me that there was more to it. Something else was eating away at him.

By now he'd almost made it to the spot where we were all waiting. That's when Billy stuck out his foot and tripped him.

The new kid went down hard, and laughter erupted from almost everyone present. Amy's face was shrouded by conflict. She seemed torn over how to react.

The new kid rolled over on his back and I could see a small trickle of blood coming down his forehead. He wiped it and then just lay there as Billy towered over him. Billy had a crazy laugh—the kind that is half laugh and half huff, when the adrenaline courses so strong that all the blood rushes from the brain to the fists. He was wild-eyed and I could tell that he was on the verge of taking it to the next level. He was in full attack mode.

I don't think I realized it at the time, but apparently I'd had enough. Perhaps all those talks from my dad about doing the right thing took over, because before I knew it, I had taken two steps toward Billy and shoved him in the chest with both hands, as hard as I could. I spat out, "Why don't you leave him alone, jerk?"

The force of my attack surprised me—and Billy too. He stumbled backward, tripped over the fire hydrant in the grass just behind him, and hit the ground harder than the other kid had.

The whole group of kids at the bus stop let out a chorus of "Ooooh!"

The adrenaline that had hijacked my body suddenly retreated, and my brain was calling the shots once again. I realized where I was and what I'd done. And all at once, I echoed their sentiment under my breath. *Ooooh.*

I think Billy was so shocked that he was having trouble finding the words to communicate what he was about to do to me. But as quickly as he went down, he sprang back up with fists clenched and a face redder than the fire hydrant he had just tripped over. In that moment, I realized that rage speaks louder than words. I was about to be pummeled.

It only took one step for him to recover the distance of my two steps—and no two-step dance was about to ensue, that was for sure. His first punch hit me square in my lip, and I could taste the warm aftermath. He had me by my shirt and was about to deliver the second blow, when out of nowhere an unfamiliar voice shouted, "David!"

We turned to find that an old white Ford station wagon had rolled to a stop at the corner while I was in my state of temporary insanity. The passenger window was rolled down and the voice was coming from a woman who quickly opened the door and began running toward us.

I recognized her. She was a lady from my dad's church, Loretta—at least I could think of her first name. I had spoken to her once or twice after services. Just niceties and such, the stuff preachers' kids are expected to say when they stand outside the front door of the church to greet everyone as they leave. I knew she had a husband and three kids, but I knew little else. She was in her late twenties with brown, naturally wavy hair that obviously went whatever direction it pleased, and apparently a very strong, domineering temperament to match.

"David! What happened?"

I was surprised she remembered my name, more so that she was running to my aid. I didn't want to be destroyed by Billy, but neither was I sure this was an appropriate escape route—the intervention of a random adult. A female-type adult, at that. A black eye or a bloody lip might be better than bruised pride.

As she drew closer, I realized she was not actually running toward me, but rather toward the new kid, who had by now managed to sit up. She knelt beside him and began examining his wounds. "David—are you hurt? Who did this to you?"

The kid did not answer. He remained stoic, staring at the ground as he'd been doing the entire time. He did not respond to Loretta's questions. He did not even seem surprised by what had just happened to him. He seemed to be just—well, blank.

Loretta stood up and demanded of the crowd, "Who did this to my little brother?"

No one said a word, but as she rotated her gaze among the dozen or so kids standing there, it didn't take long for her to see that a certain brute had me snuggly in his brutish clutches. I guess two and two were easy math at that scene.

"Oh, I get it!" she snapped. "I guess you think it's cool to pick on the new kid?"

Billy didn't answer, but I could tell by the unyielding force of his grip that his intentions toward me had not changed even the slightest bit. I guess his adrenaline reservoir had a greater capacity than mine. Besides, what were some angry woman—even though she was not small—and her crippled little brother going to do to the likes of him?

Loretta's eyes narrowed to a jagged point and she jerked her head back toward the car. There was a man behind the wheel. I had not noticed him in the melee. Apparently, neither had Billy. Mind you, this entire scene had probably only lasted a total of about forty-five seconds, though it seemed to be an eternity to the guy about to have his face smashed in. Loretta called to him. "Rod! We may need you!"

The driver's side door creaked loudly as he opened it. All I could see were his muscular shoulders as they rose above the car. He was wearing a white T-shirt with a pack of cigarettes rolled up in the left sleeve. And one behind his ear just in case it wanted a smoke. His hair was slicked back to mousy brown perfection.

Resting his right forearm on the roof of the car and tapping his fingers, he looked at Billy with "that" look—the one that says, *You have disturbed my peace. Therefore, I'm about to beat the snot out of you.*

But instead of actually saying it, he simply said, "Do we have a problem here?" His voice could have been mined straight from a gravel quarry. Loretta turned back to look at Billy and cast him that "your move" look. All other eyes followed suit. Slowly, I began to feel his grip loosen, then release.

I stepped away from him and Amy ran over to me. "David? Are you okay?"

"I'm fine," I replied. "No big deal." The pulsating pain in my lip actually did feel like a pretty big deal, and it slurred my words. She didn't seem to notice.

"David," she continued with great hesitation, "I—I didn't mean to—"

"I know." I cut her off. Her hand was on my shoulder and I took a small step away from her, moving out of her reach. She hung her head and disappeared into the protective cloud of cheerleader whispers.

Billy stormed off down the street. Rod never so much as took a step in our direction; his job was done. He simply got back into the car and shut the door. By this time, Loretta had helped her brother to his feet. He still had not spoken a word. As she helped him toward the car, she paused to study me for the first time. "Aren't you Reverend Wideman's son?"

"Yes, ma'am," I replied.

"Well, thank you so much for sticking up for my little brother. This is his first day in Liberty and I just had a feeling he might need me to check on him. You just don't understand what he's been—"

She cut off the sentence, but the look in her eyes was unnerving. Half anger. Half pity. Half terror. And anyone who knows any math at all knows that three halves do not a whole person make. I may have been only a teenager at the time, but even I could tell she had faced something of the difficult variety—and standing in the situation we were in, I had a feeling that her brother had probably been privy to it as well.

"It was nothing," I said, giving my best impression of a movie hero.

I looked at the new kid, who now stood only a few inches from me, but his head still hung low. He said nothing, not even a thank-you. But his eyes tattled on him with a moist glistening. He glanced over at the car and then took a stunted step in its direction. Loretta capitalized upon his motion and grabbed his left arm, dragging him behind her as he stumbled to catch his balance and catch up.

Awkwardly she helped him into the backseat, climbed into the front passenger side, and slammed the door. The car sped off just as the flashing yellow lights mounted atop our old school bus rose from the bottom of the hill on Hinson Street.

I picked up my scattered books and caught a glimpse of Summer. She was smiling—and just like that, my busted lip was a badge of honor.

The rest of the day was without major consequence, and after school I met up with my buddies Tim Bennett and Jeff Campbell to hang out as usual. By that time, the story of what had happened at the bus stop was folklore all across our little high school. The guys wanted a play-by-play description of the whole event. I willingly obliged.

As the afternoon sun began to wane, I made my way home. Dad's car was already in the driveway and I found him waiting for me on the front porch. Generally, this wasn't a good sign. He was still wearing his tie, but he had shed his coat. In those days, it was expected that the preacher wear a tie everywhere. To the beach, in the shower, wherever. To my dad, wearing just a tie was downright leisurely.

He was a very kind man, but as my dad he was more than willing to lower the boom, if you know what I mean.

He skipped the pleasantries. "So I hear you got into a fight today at the bus stop?"

"Yessir," I responded, my eyes combing the ground. "Um, how did you hear about that?"

It was a ridiculous question. My dad was the pastor of Liberty Manor Baptist Church. The only communication system faster than church gossip in our little town was the radio signal ferried between the Apollo astronauts and NASA headquarters in Houston. These people knew how to communicate on a whole different level of efficiency.

And when your dad is the local preacher, you learn a whole different language anyway. You actually become well-versed in a second, distinctive dialect consisting of a whole lot of "brother" this and "sister" that and "amen" to that over there. "Well, bless their heart" will suffice to set up and cover over any manner of gossip—it's the gateway phrase for any religious conversation.

In my head, I could just imagine how it went down. It was probably "Sister" Margaret Thornton who spilled the beans. I bet she could barely balance that bluish beehive she called a hairdo on her head as she waved her index finger back and forth like a clock pendulum. "Brother Wideman, what a great sermon you spake unto us on Sunday. Amen and amen to all of that. But listen, a little songbird told me that your boy, David, up and hit another kid at the bus stop today, bless his heart. Do you really think that sort of behavior is becoming of a godly young man, much less a pastor's son?"

Dad answered me with, "Well, I had a visitor today at the church office."

I bet you did, I thought to myself.

He continued, “It was Loretta Ward. She told me what you did to stick up for her brother.”

“Oh.” It was all I could think to say. The look in my dad’s eye was not at all what I had expected. He was solemn, but not in a disappointed way. Could that be a little pride I was detecting?

“Son, I want you to know that, as a rule, I do not condone fighting—”

“I know, I know,” I cut him off. “It was just that the kid couldn’t really—”

“Let me finish, son. I was going to say that even though I do not condone fighting, I think what you did today was the right thing.”

“You do?”

“Yes. You know, when we see something that we know to be wrong and we have the power to fix it, we should—well, fix it. Otherwise, we just become part of the problem. You don’t have to be throwing punches to be the bad guy. Sometimes good guys are the bad guys because they are afraid to do the right thing when the situation calls for it. What you did today was right.”

He put his hand on my shoulder and smiled with a smile I’d never seen before from him. It was an adult smile. It was as if he were talking to someone with maturity. I could feel my chest involuntarily poke out a bit.

He chuckled a little and then continued. “On the other hand, son, sometimes it’s easier to fight for something in a moment of passion than it is to stick with something worth fighting for over the long haul.”

Uh-oh. This didn’t sound good at all. He had that tone to his voice that usually landed me a job raking the yard of an elderly church lady or washing all the dirty dishes after dinner.

He continued, "Loretta's family is desperate. You see, her brother David just moved here from St. Louis. David—well, his mom died of cancer."

"Dad?" I interrupted. "What's—you know—wrong with him?" I tried to ask in a way that wouldn't sound like I had noticed anything wrong with him at all.

My dad, of course, picked up on it quickly. "It's okay, son. David does have problems. He has a disorder called cerebral palsy."

"Is he retarded?" I asked.

"No, not at all. Nothing is wrong with his brain except that his body and mouth don't know how to catch up with it."

"Oh," I replied. I sat there pondering his answer for a moment. These were new channels of conversation between the two of us.

Dad continued, "Listen, David. As I was telling you, that family is desperate because, ever since his mom died, he won't talk to anybody. He doesn't have any friends. He doesn't even seem like he wants to live anymore. Loretta is at her wit's end. She asked me if you might mind coming over tomorrow and try talking to him. You know, since you were the one who took up for him today."

"Me?" It was all I said out loud, but on the inside I thought about the ancient truth that no good deed goes unpunished. I held my tongue, but I guess my expression gave me away.

Dad regained his familiar father tone, the one that let me know we were no longer talking adult to adult. "Now, son, I know this is not easy, but remember what we talked about. Someone worth fighting for is someone worth living for too. David Ring needs a friend and I know that David Wideman is the best one around."

There was no fighting it. I loved my dad too much to protest. "Okay, Dad. I'll try."

He gave me a small hug and we went inside for supper. But all through the evening, I kept thinking about the new kid, especially every time I felt my fat lip. I was not looking forward to the next day, mainly because it was Saturday and this little mission I had been placed on would most certainly put a crimp in my plans for basketball with the guys.

I resigned myself to go do what I had committed to do, even though we had nothing in common—or at least that's what I thought at the time.

Nothing, that is, besides the name David.

3

October 28, 1953

"We're losing her."

I can imagine the doctor's face: red but determined. He would remember his training in medical school—and it would seem insufficient. What could ever prepare a man for such a moment? He was supposed to be the calm one. The strong one. The one to never panic. But his expression wasn't doing him any favors with the nurses. They knew his face was saying it all.

This one was probably not going to make it.

Oscar Ring's whole world had been reduced to one sharp fear. He paced the waiting room floor at St. Bernard's Hospital, waiting for news. It was a modest medical facility, as would be expected in Jonesboro, Arkansas. As he threatened to carve a ditch in the dirty tile with his incessant walking, he once again reached the window and looked out across the street from his third-floor vantage point.

There was a huge cross atop Central Baptist Church. It was white and it fully captured his eye. He felt a fleeting peace and courage, but these emotions couldn't take hold. Not as he thought of her. She was the one who needed strength right now.

"Oh God, please be with Leron," he muttered. "Please." He held his small hat in his hand, once black but now faded into a color for which there was no name. His work hat.

This particular hospital was the destination of the locals for everyday medical needs. Most trauma or major surgeries would make their way east to Memphis across the huge bridge—a modern engineering spectacle that spanned the mighty Mississippi and joined Tennessee and Arkansas.

The speed of St. Bernard's was more suited for the occasional case of flu or a sting from a yellow jacket.

Leron Ring's case was far more complex and dangerous.

Yellow jackets are strange little critters. Their yellow and black colors fool a lot of folks into thinking they are bees. But they are actually wasps. You can tell because yellow jackets are thin-waisted. Bees are thick-waisted. The other huge difference is that bees can only sting a person one time. Yellow jackets, on the other hand, can sting more than once and often attack in groups when their nests are disturbed. If someone is allergic, their gang attacks can be deadly.

It almost seemed as if Leron Ring had disturbed some nest of yellow jackets and couldn't escape the numerous stings.

When she found out she was pregnant, she was hopeful that this baby would dodge the diagnosis of his three older brothers. They were her boys and she loved them dearly. Three sons, three cases of hemophilia. But even more than that, she hoped this child would survive. Besides her three boys and four daughters, she had lost three others. Two stillbirths.

The other was a twin to her daughter Loretta and had died soon after being born.

Her seven children—soon to be eight—had been born in two distinct groups separated by quite a few years. The first five, Gilbert, Leon, Bernice, Bonnie, and Loretta, were born between 1927 and 1939. The younger two, Willard and Judy, were born in 1945 and 1951. So her oldest son was old enough to be her youngest daughter's father. This age difference vastly separated the two sets of children, making them very little like siblings. Nevertheless, all her boys had been born with diseased blood.

But it was her own blood that was now pooling on the tile of the delivery room floor, its bright red staining the sterile squares. She was severely hemorrhaging and was barely holding on to consciousness.

Her face was as pale as a dry bone. Her lips lost their color, their life. The medical staff scurried about. She turned to the nurse closest to her, only one question on her mind. She whispered out a faint gasp that somehow echoed louder than the shouting of orders and the clanging of stainless steel instruments on stainless steel trays.

"Baby?"

The nurse didn't have the courage to answer her. She looked away and reengaged in her task at hand, pretending she hadn't heard the question. But she gave her reply without realizing it as she glanced over at a table near the back wall of the room.

No words were necessary.

Leron's eyes followed the nurse's to the table. It held a bundle of white cloth stained with streaks of red. Unattended to. Motionless. Lifeless.

"No! My baby!"

The realization of death brought a new intensity of life for Leron. Desperate, raging life. She convulsed hard against the efforts of the doctors and nurses to restrain her.

"Hold her still, for God's sake!" The doctor was drenched in sweat. It stung his eyes, but he could not stop to wipe it. This was it. Any more blood lost and this woman would be joining her new son. He looked up at the nurse nearest Leron's head and gave her an accusing look. *How could you let her know?*

It was the kind of mother's intuition no one would wish for.

The doctor dispensed with the kindly bedside manner. "Leron! You have to calm down right now!" He'd already lost another one of Leron's babies. Not Leron too. Not today.

But Leron continued to thrash, unabated. She was a woman on fire. She could not have a third stillborn child. She would not accept it.

Soon the loss of blood stole her strength again. She slowly began to calm down, not as one who was recovering but as one who was giving up, dying. She no longer felt the pain of the doctor's sharp instruments. She felt nothing. Heard nothing.

She just laid her head back, face turned toward the table where her precious little one's body was still lying. White stillness began to creep in from the corners and peripheries. This was it. She was ready to go. Why would anyone want to stay here? It was too much to bear.

As she began to drift away, she whispered one final word, "Jesus." Her eyes remained open, but lost their focus. Fading. The doctors and nurses began slowing down their frantic actions to save her. It was a lost cause, and they watched her life drain away.

The doctor looked at his watch. "Time of death is 1:50 a.m." Then he reached up to close her eyes.

But as he did, they suddenly blinked. He jerked back from her as if he had seen a ghost. Her eyes were focused again. "My baby," she whispered. "He just moved."

Against their best logic, everyone in the room turned to look at the little table in the corner. The little bundle was motionless. Then Leron suddenly convulsed again, and screamed, "There he went again! Did you see it?"

The doctor locked eyes with the nurse and motioned with his head toward the little table. The nurse knew her task; she would remove the poor, broken body, the reminder of all that is cruel and hopeless in life. Maybe the mother's delusions could be so easily put away.

The nurse stood over the little bundle that had been lifeless for almost twenty minutes. As she put her hands upon the blanket to pick up his body, she heard something.

But of course that was impossible. The tiny, desperate sound meant the nurse was imagining things too.

Except that she heard it again.

"Doctor, this baby is moving!"

Leron erupted with a sound that was somewhere between a laugh and a scream. The rest of the room was roused almost as dramatically. Doctors and nurses began flooding in to assist. This was more than improbable; it was impossible. But it was happening right before their eyes.

Given a new reason to live, Leron began to fight again. The delivering doctor went back to caring for her. "I think the bleeding has stopped," he said, shaking his head at the turn of events all around.

But the rest of the crew went to work on the little baby who had been lying there with no breath. No heartbeat. They converged on him, poking and prodding. They helped him breathe. For the first time in his young life, the infant began to put up a fight.

It would not be the last occasion. Not even close.

Leron drifted into a restful darkness, her emotional and physical strength spent. When her eyes opened again, the traumatic memories were just out of her grasp. She saw nothing but white, but she wasn't in heaven; the sharp abdominal pain ruled that one out. Exactly where was she?

Finally she could make out her own toes pushing up the white blanket at the end of her bed.

It was a hospital blanket.

Consciousness and clarity began seeping back into her mind in measured doses, but she was still groggy from the anesthesia. Her thoughts wandered through the most random of things. Had she left the stove on at the house? Where was Oscar, and were his shirts ironed? What room was this? Where was everyone else?

Then it hit her.

"My baby!"

Her cries immediately brought the nightshift nurse running into the room. She was a pretty young nurse as redheaded as a brushfire. She looked as if a single moment in the sun might leave permanent grill marks on her creamy skin, so pale that her face would betray her in any moment of even the slightest stressor. At this moment her cheeks glowed hot, but Leron didn't seem to notice or care. She kept screaming like a mad woman.

"Now Mrs. Ring! You gonna have to pipe down, sweetie!" The nurse's accent was vintage Arkansas. "We got yo' baby and we taking good care of him."

Leron's eyes filled with tears, washing away both the cobwebs and the unimaginable pain from her heart. "It's a miracle! He's alive!"

"Yes ma'am, he is. And if I hadn't been here to see it, I reckon I wouldn't believe it."

"Oh Jesus! Thank you, Jesus!" Leron closed her eyes and rocked back and forth. She put both hands over her heart as if it might come out of her chest if she didn't. "Can I hold him? Can I hold my baby?"

The nurse gave no reply. Instead she went about her business, checking the IV and adjusting the bed pillows. Leron detected everything she wasn't saying. After all, she was a mother complete with all the intuition that role entails. But instead of asking again, she simply focused her glare on the nurse, compelling an answer.

The nurse finally took a deep breath and looked her in the eyes. Her tone was touched with a sympathy designed not to stifle the new hope in this woman. "Mrs. Ring, I'd love nothing more than to bring that precious boy in here and let you rock him, but the doctor has him in the ICU, just like you are. They are monitoring him closely."

"But he's gonna be okay, right? You said he was alive, so he's gonna be okay?"

"He is alive. And there's no denying that's a miracle. But you gotta understand something. That poor baby done lay there on that table not breathing for over eighteen minutes. That's a long time to go without oxygen."

Leron went blank. The nurse hated offering the kind of bad news that doctors were usually looked upon to serve up, but she admired the courage of this fighting mother.

First hours passed, then a few days. Eventually the doctor came to see Leron, but he was enigmatic at best in his reports on the baby. All she could gather was that he was in the ICU. She didn't feel like a woman who had almost died earlier that week. She was full of vigor and spunk, relentlessly hounding the entire hospital staff with a singular question: when she could hold her miracle child. But no one would give her a straight answer.

Three days after he was born, the moment finally came. The doctor himself brought Leron's precious bundle into the room and laid him in her arms. His face was ruddy with life and breath. Every gurgle, every twitch, every belabored breath was music to her ears. Leron gently touched the top of his soft head, caressing the few hairs he had. He seemed to respond to her, though she couldn't see it with her eyes. It was something she could feel—he knew his mother's touch, and he needed it.

The doctor had been talking the whole time, but she had not heard a word. Finally, he got her attention. "Mrs. Ring, we are about to let your husband come see both of you. But I hope you understand what I've been telling you. We don't know how the lack of oxygen may have affected your baby. There's no way to tell. There could be no effects, or it could be severe."

She tore her gaze away from his beautiful face and locked eyes with the doctor. "Severe?"

He took a deep breath. "Yes ma'am. He may never walk or talk as he should. He may never be—well, normal."

Leron took a deep breath, the kind one takes before boarding a train to go fight in a war that has no perceivable end in sight. She knew what this meant, and in that moment her heart decided.

She smiled at the doctor. "Thank you for working so hard to save my baby. I mean, really, thank you so much. And I understand what you're saying."

She paused for a moment to gather herself. But the doctor perceived something peculiar about her in such a solemn moment. He had seen any number of mothers hold flawed infants such as this one. He had seen the tears form, the resigned love laden with grief. But this was no such scene. This was a mother holding her perfect child.

It wasn't sorrow that held back her words, it was joy. Deep and powerful, unmixed with any other emotion—yet not a cheap, delusional happiness. This was the powerful joy that could stare down harsh reality without flinching. There was not a hint of sadness or regret to be found.

"I don't want him to be normal," she said, looking up at the doctor. "God saved him. He was dead and now he is alive. He is not made to be normal."

The young nurse was present, and this was all too much for her. Her pale complexion was now completely blushed and drenched in tears. Even the normally stoic and professional doctor, veteran of many emotional battlefields, wiped his eyes with his fingertips. It was the kind of move that could be mistaken for wiping the sleepiness away after a long twelve-hour shift. But he gave himself away when he then dried his fingers on his lab coat.

His countenance was now incredibly soft. "This boy is going to need a mother like you. He is going to need constant care. Constant help. He will have a lot of giants to face in his life."

Leron continued to watch her precious little miracle. She stroked his red cheek gently. He gurgled about and blinked a few times as he struggled to open his squinted eyes. But she could tell he was looking at her. Mother and child forged their bond.

"If he will face giants, then I guess I'll call him David."

4

September 1969

The sidewalk seemed to be a million miles long.

As a pastor's son, I was used to doing things that made me uncomfortable. This life came with a built-in spotlight. And many times, that light was enough to make a kid sweat profusely. Goldfish have more privacy than preachers' kids. Parishioners could cash in their all-access pass to see everything from our sock drawers to our kitchen floors. After all, they paid for our house, right?

They should have just installed one of those machines with the coin slot, like the one on the mechanical horse down at the Five and Dime. Only a nickel to see straight into a family's home. Ask anything you want; you're paying for it. When the light comes on, take a good gander!

But this light seemed hotter than the others. I was heading to the home of a kid about whom I knew nothing except that he was miserable. What was I going to say? What was he going to say? Heck, what if he didn't say anything at all? I should have just left well enough alone. My lip would feel better soon, that was for sure.

But deep inside, I knew my soul would not. I guess I got that from my dad. That feeling when you know you wouldn't feel right doing anything but—well, what feels right.

Dad never seemed to mind the spotlight. He never held the coin slot in contempt. He just soldiered on and smiled, remaining patient with those who invaded our space.

I've often heard of preachers' kids who hate their parents or the ministry or even God because the light was just too bright and they got burnt. They fled from what they were raised to believe, lashing out against the light for the rest of their lives. When wounds are that deep, I suppose no salve can ease the blisters.

But I never felt that way about our life. My dad was not bitter and neither did he ever allow the light to get out of hand. Sure, we might sweat a bit. But he also kept us hidden in his shadow when need be, and we were happy there too. That was Dad.

The leaves continued to make their music beneath my feet, signaling that I was coming. Unprepared for sure, but coming nonetheless. Ready or not. Mostly not.

The sidewalk eventually led me to an old, white mailbox dotted with rust spots, faded, hand-painted numbers barely discernible beneath the layer of dust. 191. I turned left and began walking down the long, dirty, paved driveway leading to Loretta Ward's house.

The building was modest but not quaint. After all, Loretta and Rod had three kids of their own. The paint was a pale yellow that was chipping in places, but it was only noticeable when you got close to the house. I guess from the distance of the street, all of our houses looked different.

I was nearly to the front steps. There were eleven of them, more than you would think for a house that size. They were concrete, spider-webbed with cracks, and led up to a very small concrete porch. In only a moment, it seemed, I stood before an old, beaten-up storm door with the screen ripped in places. The slats of the wood frame ran like a cross through the door, creating a place for the screen to be tacked down. This made two squares at the top of the door—like two square eyes atop a face.

There was no reason to delay the inevitable, so I reached up and knocked on its nose. I could hear the rustle of children inside. More like screaming, actually. Not real screaming, just the normal screaming that accompanies toddlers and small children. It was that wild concoction of childhood delight and immature whininess shaken, not stirred, into an elixir only parents know well.

Loretta answered the door, her hair pulled back and covered with a blue handkerchief, and by the look on her face she had been chugging that elixir all day. By the sound of the melee around her, who could blame her for looking exhausted?

"David!" She gave her best effort at a smile. "Thank you so much for coming over. Come right on in."

I crossed over the threshold just as a small blond banshee whisked past me at the speed of sound, nearly causing me to lose my balance. The high-pitched noise was deceptive because it turned out the little animal was male. He couldn't have been older than three and he was screaming in piercing tones. "Mama! Mama! Ouchy! Brudder give me ouchy!"

Loretta's face suddenly dropped its mask and revealed the mom beneath. "Jacob Fredrick Ward! What did you do to your brother!"

"But, Mom! He started it!" The voice came from the other room. Or another galaxy. It was hard to tell.

"You march your butt in that kitchen and eat dinner, or you're going to get it when your dad gets home!" There was a certain wildness in her eyes. I looked down, embarrassed for myself and for them. We did not yell like this at home. Oh, we yelled—just not like this. I wasn't sure how I could tell the difference, but I could.

"Well, are you ready?"

I realized she was talking to me. Loretta was back to her front door self—the one with the smile. The speed of her transformation was astounding. "Yes, ma'am," I replied. I was ready to get this over with.

"His room is down in the basement. When our mom died, I guess—I guess we just didn't have any other rooms to . . ." She was trailing off into a sad place.

"I wish I could live in our basement. That's the biggest room in our whole house." My attempt to comfort her seemed to do the trick, and a small smile crept across her face.

"Thank you for that, David. Come on. I'll show you the way."

We walked through the kitchen and past a small table where three little kids sat playing with their respective bowls of spaghetti. The marinara and noodles were making short work of the white of their faces. They were covered in the stuff, but at least there was quiet.

As we walked past, I noticed that another person—an adult—was seated there too. She was a blonde. She was sitting down so I really couldn't tell how tall she was, but by the looks of her face she was thin. Very thin. She seemed to be about the same age as Loretta—somewhere in her twenties, but more attractive.

She was staring down at a small bowl of cereal, slowly swirling it about with one of the kids' spoons. It was as if she were looking through to the floor beneath, completely oblivious to the mayhem of children all around her.

Loretta must have seen that I noticed her. "Oh, sorry, David. I almost forgot. This is my best friend from high school, Debbie. She's staying with us for a while."

"Oh," I said, expecting some kind of response from Debbie. None came. She kept looking down as if we weren't there.

"Debbie!" Loretta touched her shoulder hard enough that her trance was broken.

"Oh, I'm so sorry!" She looked up at me. "Oh . . ." Maybe it was just my imagination, but her eyes seemed to come to life a bit when she saw me. I wasn't real sure what to make of it, since she was a grown woman.

"David Wideman," I said as politely as a choirboy, extending my hand toward her. She gently shook it and I let go as quickly as possible. Thankfully, it was obvious that Loretta was moving us along to the business at hand, so I was able to turn back toward the basement door and keep walking.

Just past the table was a small glass sliding door. It had a single crack at the bottom left corner that meandered around like a river on a map, no doubt the result of a toy going airborne or a rock fight that tried to make its way indoors. Through this door, I could see the backyard. The reds and oranges of the trees invited me to keep walking and make my escape, but I knew that was no serious option. And that was okay. I was a Wideman and facing our fears was a family birthright.

Just to the right of the back door was another door. A smaller one. Loretta opened it, and I stood at the threshold and stared downward into what seemed like mostly darkness, save a lone hanging bulb that moved back and forth ever so slowly and illuminated the two-by-four stick-built staircase that led into the basement.

"He's down there," Loretta said.

There were so many things I wanted to ask in reply. Down there in the dark? By himself? What is he, some kind of animal? And you are asking me to walk down there alone?

Instead all that came up from my inner recesses was "Okay." And thus I began my slow descent into the darkness to find David Ring.

The stairs creaked with each step, accenting my short trip down with the sound of emotional violins out of tune. When I reached the bottom, I was literally standing in darkness.

"Hello?"

There was no answer.

"Are you down here?"

No voice answered mine. But I was suddenly unnerved by the distinct sound of breathing. I rubbed my hand up and down the rough block wall just to my left and finally I found it—the light switch. The click was the most welcome sound I had heard all day; in an instant, the darkness of the room fled.

The floor was a charcoal gray, typical basement concrete. Smooth and dusty, with white water spots in the corners. A large, well-worn rug covered the center of the floor. It was auburn and blue, or had been at one time. An old chest of drawers was positioned in the corner of the room, held up by three good legs and a stack of old books.

A small cast iron bed was offset on the same wall as the chest of drawers. The blanket that covered it seemed an oddity to me—blue, dotted with large white circles. Obviously one of the children's blankets.

Then my eyes saw him, sitting on the bed. Alone. He was like a downed tree in the middle of a snowy meadow. He didn't belong here and his presence exclaimed the fact. It also suggested there was a long story behind his coming to this moment.

"David?" I asked with hesitation. He didn't look up at me. "I don't know if you remember me, but I was at the bus stop the other day when you and Billy—you know . . ." I wasn't sure how to say it. When Billy made a fool out of you? When I got the snot beaten out of me? When your sister saved us both?

I abandoned the phrase. This was awkward; he just sat in his place, and I just stood there. There seemed to be a whole watermelon stuck in my throat. *Thanks Dad*, I thought to myself. *Terrific idea you had.*

"I wemembuh you."

I looked up quickly. Even though he spoke with an obvious impediment, it was a relief to hear his voice. It was good to know one of us could still talk.

He continued. "Why aw yuh heuh?"

I wasn't sure how to answer. I guess if you're sitting alone in a dark basement and some guy you don't really know walks down your steps and turns on the lights, you do have that question.

"I just wanted to stop by and say hi, I guess."

"Yo' thuh pweacha's boy?" His belabored tone made it hard to tell if his words were a question or an accusation. I noticed now how each word seemed to take concerted energy to speak. The impediment seemed to control more than his language; it dominated every part of his physical presence.

I started to answer him, but he overrode my attempt. "Yuh shouldn't have come heuh—yo' daddy made yuh do it." His *it* sounded more like three words than one. More like ii-ah-t.

In that moment, I developed my first conclusion about David Ring—and it was one that many people probably would have never opened their minds to even consider. I guess you could say David himself pried open my mind and made sure the truth of things got into me. This truth was: *He looks a certain way and he sounds a certain way—but that has nothing to do with his intelligence.*

He had figured me out before I'd ever said more than a few words. Yes, my father had made me come to this creepy basement. No, I would never have chosen to come on my own. How strange that this boy could use such slurred speech to speak such a sharp observation.

"That's not the only reason I came," I said. It was a poor attempt to save face, but it was the best one I could muster.

He seemed not to care whether I stayed or left. And given how hard this was for me anyway, I was ticked off about that.

"You know what? Think whatever you want about me. I didn't do anything to you!"

My own boldness surprised me. I think it surprised him too. He actually looked up. My words had broken his staring contest with the floor.

I guess you never really see people until you see their eyes.

His were blue. Very blue. Like the crystalline turquoise of a tropical Caribbean bay I had seen in my Dad's *National Geographic* magazines. They peered out at me from beneath a fairly thick brow, especially for someone our age. Natural hairy frown lines.

He was actually a good-looking kid. When he wasn't speaking and his eyes were uplifted, the painful struggle seemed to subside for just a moment.

"Fine. Go 'head and weave wike evwyone ewse."

"I'm here, ain't I? You act like you want me to leave!"

"It doesn't mattuh. I don' even know yuh anyway." I could still see the blue, but it had faded.

A new silence ensued, but this one was more tolerable. It was like that feeling in the air when a storm has finally released its fury. There may be some carnage, but the air feels lighter.

Truth was, I liked the fact that David had a little spunk in him. It's hard to talk to a wall. We hadn't said much and most of it was either awkward or heated, but for teenage boys, a little blood drawn was a good thing. It cleared the air. It set borders that each of us now knew and understood. It probably wouldn't matter, but at least we had been able to spar with each other—and I knew there was more to him than what I had seen at the bus stop.

Above all else, I felt that my obligation had been met. Dad would not expect more than what I had attempted. I could return home with a clear conscience, knowing that this guy wasn't looking for anything but a dark room for being alone in. If that was all he wanted, who could stop him?

"Well," I said, turning back toward the stairs, "I guess if you ever want to hang out and do anything, you know where to find me." The words were more inviting than the actual tone. It was a classic teenager move. Say one thing, but scream another. I started back toward the steps.

"Wayeeet."

I paused and turned around. He was just sitting there, staring at me. His left hand was limply outstretched toward me and his fingers had an awkward draw to them, no doubt another fruit of his disorder. He kept his mouth slightly open, but it seemed as if his tongue had suddenly been struck with paralysis. It was not as if he was trying to decide if he should say something else. It was more like he was completely incapable of saying another solitary word.

It was one of those moments in life when you rapidly grow up by several years in just a few seconds, though I suppose it's not as sudden as it seems. Everything that abruptly bloomed inside of me had been planted there for years by my parents. I guess you can't sit around and watch fruit on a tree grow. You just walk outside one day to find that there are apples on the branches.

As he was frozen in that position, reaching out to me, I entered my own frozen state. What had been a fleeting moment of courage at the bus stop was now becoming part of my lifeblood. The reluctant walk down the sidewalk that had led me here—even the angry words I had just hurled at this resistant human wall—it all began to come together inside me.

His one word took hold of me. *Wait*. He needed me to wait. He needed.

"Do you like root beer?"

The words seemed to leave my mouth before I even thought them up. *Did I just say that?* He lowered his hand and closed his mouth. He still said nothing, but he began to rock, and shifted his way off the bed to drag his body toward the steps where I was standing. Acting as if I were not even there, he brushed past me and began the long ascent.

It was the first time I'd ever seen someone with cerebral palsy climb stairs. Nor had I even thought about it. This was a lengthy endeavor—and I began to realize that everything was like this for him. He was my age, but he was not like me. Not yet. I guess not ever. But somehow I felt a need to balance the scales between us. To see them not tipped so cruelly to one side.

I may not have been limping as he was, but I was certainly limiting myself to his speed. Since I was waiting for him to get there first, I was matching his pace. When we were about halfway up the steps, Loretta came to the doorway at the top. The look on her face was inconclusive at best. She seemed surprised that we were coming up together, but I couldn't tell if there was any relief mixed in. She just stood there and watched us—and we were quite the climbing duo.

It seemed like half an hour passed before we emerged from the darkness of that basement together. David grabbed his jacket and walked out the front door. Loretta looked at me in confusion.

"Um—I think we're going to Begg's for some root beer?"

It was more a question than a statement. Loretta's eyes widened and she began scrambling to grab her purse on the kitchen table.

"Oh! Okay then. Well, here's a few quarters for you guys." She placed the coins in my right hand, and then used her other hand to close my fist, holding it there for a second. Just a touch of moisture showed about the edges of her eyes. "You just don't know what this means," she whispered in my ear. "He has no friends. At all."

Then her grip tightened significantly, so much so that I began to squirm a bit, both from the pain and the implication that I was his friend. I was willing to give the latter a go, but it was by no means a sure thing. Trying not to seem too rude, I gently pulled my hand away and simply said, "Yes, ma'am."

Surprisingly, I had to jog a little bit to catch up with David. He did better with sidewalks than stairs. I fell into step with him and we were on our way. Not more than one car slowed down as it passed us, though I was self-conscious. I guess we were quite the pair to behold. He still was not talking to me, but at least we were moving.

About ten minutes in, he found his tongue. "I know yo' thuh pweacha's boy, but what's yo' name?"

"Wideman. David Wideman."

His face brightened. I wouldn't call it a smile, but it was the furthest thing from frown I had seen so far. "Like meh?"

"Yep. David—just like you." The idea was more than a little funny to me—that I would have ever been able to look at this person and utter the words *just like you*.

I continued, "But you know what? All this David stuff is going to make things confusing. We need to make things easier."

He stopped and looked closely at me. "What do you mean?"

"Well, how about instead of calling each other by the same name—how about I just call you Ring instead?"

"Wing, huh?" I couldn't read his thoughts, but I could only imagine how many unwanted nicknames had been hurled at him over the years by various bullies. He clearly kept thinking about it, but my mind was made up. Every boy needs someone to give him a nickname. A real nickname. It doesn't have to be fancy. It can just be a shortened version of his real name, like Dave, or it can have a "y" added to the end, like Johnny or Jimmy. It just means that someone cares enough to give their own spin to a name.

I interrupted his thoughts. "Yep, that's what I'm going to do. From now on, I'll just call you Ring."

He looked at me, and for a moment I thought I saw a mischievous grin peek out from behind his lips. But like an unexpected rainbow in the spray of the water hose, it was gone as quickly as it came.

5

Spring 1955

"God will never leave you nor forsake you!"

There were no "amens," only the fanning of various pieces of paper from sweaty old women. All that flapping was almost visually overstimulating from the preacher's vantage point on the small stage.

Oscar Ring knew his small congregation was much more concerned with degrees than divinity. Still he pushed on through his text, this week taken from the book of Joshua. It was just like all the other sermons he had preached for the past several months. His words were fresh and compelling, but his spirit was barren and dry. He wondered if the people could tell. He doubted that they cared one way or another—as long as their wrist-powered air conditioners didn't break down.

He was preaching about Joshua and God's words to him just before setting out into a Promised Land filled with milk and honey. But to the one leading the army, there were more pressing matters. This land was also filled with giants. Warriors. Killers.

"Be strong and of good courage."

He wished he felt strong or courageous. Weak and weary might have been a more accurate description of his current condition. But that message didn't sell too well in a Southern pulpit.

Times in northeast Arkansas were tough for everyone, preachers included. The nearest city was Jonesboro, and even it was not a huge town. It was located about an hour west of the Mississippi River, just opposite Memphis. Big enough to catch your attention, but not big enough to keep it very long. It was like the opening geographical act for Arkansas's main event. If you kept driving, you'd find majestic mountain ranges and natural hot springs to write home about. But if you didn't pay attention, this flat, often flooded landscape would slide right out of your memory.

This land was delta. Well, technically it was a ridge, but it was close to the delta.

Life here revolved around two things: soybeans and cotton. For the Ring family and most of the families they knew, cotton was the king and soybeans were the very powerful queen, not to be dismissed or trifled with. But cotton still ruled, and each ball of fibrous white was grown, handpicked, and bagged in those fields by the millions. But nearly none of the black or white hands that picked it ever saw the millions made from it. The color of the hand did not change the way it calloused. This was poor country.

Which didn't mean it wasn't good country, if only to those who lived there. The funny thing about poverty is that sometimes those living in the middle of it can be richer than those looking down at it from the outside. If there is enough food to eat, a little roof overhead, and endless miles of fields to work and play in (even if they aren't yours), then life itself can be as rich as pockets are empty.

Times kept changing in Arkansas, and for the most part those pockets stayed pretty empty for most folks. In the old days, people worked beside each other for hours on end beneath the blistering sun. They would drink from the same dipper when the water bucket came around—as if it represented the experience they were all guzzling just as long as the sun stung them with its heat.

White or black—it didn't matter so much. Though racism was very much alive and kicking, cotton itself in Arkansas had no prejudices. Perhaps it was dangerous to be black in certain towns after dark, but in the light of day, any individual was just a worker, regardless of his or her color. Manual labor in the fields was always manual labor, even when much of the process was displaced by the rise of cotton gins and other machinery. Combines and hay binds and cotton picking machines—make no mistake, there was no "cotton pickin'" way that these people ever stopped working just because machines started doing so.

All these machines did was increase the fields' yields by exponential levels, thus making northeast Arkansas one of the newest palaces for old King Cotton—the new South living just a little westward. Even if a machine was not technically manually operated, it still took someone's manual operation to fuel it, position it, run it, and then inevitably fix it when it broke down—all the time. Many men spent many hours fixing these machines, forever proving that when it came to cotton in delta country, there was always plenty of work to do for those willing to drink of the humid air around them.

Jonesboro sat up on what was known as Crowley's Ridge, which ran all the way from southeastern Missouri to the Mississippi River near Helena. It was so named because of Benjamin Crowley, the first European to find the area around 1820. It was not the most famous part of the country, or even of Arkansas, yet it was not without consequence. It was the site of a Civil War battle, the Battle of Chalk Bluff in 1863. It was a tactical victory for the Confederacy, but a costly one that left Brigadier General John Marmaduke's imposing cavalry decimated, forcing him to abandon his second expedition into Missouri.

At Helena, Union troops placed cannons on the ridge, which commanded a view of the Mississippi River. From that vantage point, any Rebel boat trying to move upstream or down could be destroyed. These were not incidents of the War Between the States that most citizens, or even historians, would remember or probably even recognize. Much like the ridge itself, it left little impression on the landscape or on history.

As the years rolled on, more land was bought up. Settled. Farmed. The roads intersected one another in hard right angles, carving the land into perfect squares defined by old stone walls, fences, and canals to water the fields. Vast fields. To stand at a four-way intersection and gaze down any of the roads in any direction was to stare into the vastness of infinity. The square fields seemed to go on forever—not necessarily the most unique or striking geography, but home nonetheless to a steady people and a steady way of life.

The landscape was not just flat, it was also bare. Those views of infinite straight-lined roads corralling equally infinite squares of green fields were easy to see because hardly any trees blocked the view. Since settlers had first arrived in the delta area and Crowley's Ridge, they set themselves on a mission to clear-cut the land. The river flooding had created a rich and deep soil perfect for growing cotton, and the trees were in the way of this white gold mine that stretched across the plain as far as the eye could see.

So, especially after the Civil War, people continued clearing the forests of the delta, channeling its rivers and draining its swamps to create more agricultural land. When it was all said and done, the landscape of eastern Arkansas was transformed, with ninety percent of its forests cleared away to make room for King Cotton—and all his many Southern and Midwestern servants.

All this flooded land also produced the growth of another product rivaling the cotton and the soybeans: mosquitoes. They seemed to thrive in—even feed upon—the intense humidity. The clouds of steam that Arkansans breathed and sweated in were what the people just called air. But one could seek temporary refuge from both of these irritants by heading down to one of the country stores that had sprung up in little towns surrounding Jonesboro: Paragould, Marked Tree, and even towns further east like Blytheville and Osceola.

The stores had big screen doors to banish the mosquitoes while admitting the breeze. These were often decorated with painted aluminum advertisements—signs for bread companies, most of them, in yellows and whites and blues and reds, meticulously painted, with catchy (and not so catchy) slogans for Wonder Bread, Colonial, or Sunbeam and images of young girls and boys smiling and eating pieces of bread, beckoning the overheated individual to come inside for some food or refreshment.

Once inside the store, one could find surefire relief from the blistering heat by rustling up a few dimes and cozying up to the Coca-Cola machine in the corner next to the pot-bellied coal stove. It immediately stood out to everyone who came through the door. How could someone miss the classic Coke red with its signature white cursive writing? It beckoned the thirsty to partake—and oddly enough, probably become thirstier once a drink had been consumed. It was an ingenious ploy: draw in the thirsty and then quench their thirst with something that increased their thirst—and do it one dime at a time.

When money was deposited in the machine, the glass bottle moved down from the top to the dispenser in a zigzag motion—as entertaining to little sweaty boys and girls as any pinball machine out there. Or at least that's what they told themselves, because there were no pinball machines in those parts for comparison. Some Arkansans even had certain special traditions with their Cokes that would probably make Northerners run for cover beneath their snowdrifts, such as dropping a small pack of peanuts into their Coke, producing a fizzy, salty-sweet summer concoction. One man's never is another man's nectar.

And if there were no rocking chairs for sitting and sipping whatever version of soda had been purchased and doctored, the store usually had ample stacks of full tow sacks that would suffice. These were burlap bags used for transporting coffee, wheat, corn, potatoes, or any other sundry dry good one could think of. Others called them gunnysacks, but not here in Arkansas. They were tow sacks. They were seats.

The sacks were useful for all sorts of things, but contrary to what people often thought and wrote about poor women in the South, no one around those parts had ever seen someone wearing a tow sack as a dress. That was nothing but a Yankee legend. The burlap was too coarse to be pressed up against soft skin—and in the land of cotton, there were plenty of less abrasive options for clothing.

All the flooding and open fields sent an open invitation for ducks to fly in by the millions—and duck hunters would follow. The area was now a paradise for camouflaged men; dads, brothers, sons, and nephews spent a few days a year hiding in a blind and skipping showers. After all, what more does a man want in life than to sacrifice personal hygiene for the thrill of the hunt?

Oscar Ring was in a blind of his own, but it wasn't for sport. He looked out at his congregation and let his mouth, not his heart, continue to do the talking, but he knew everything was about to change. He was no Joshua, much as he had once aspired to be. He had been marching around his own private Jericho for several years now, but those lofty, fortified walls were still as high and daunting as they had been when he started.

He loved his family, but it had seen some rough times. He loved his wife, Leron, dearly, but her babies' stillbirths had almost done her in.

Leron had always been tough, but now it was a different kind of tough—one that was coolly pushing him to the outside. Sometimes he wondered if she would ever be the same. And then he would feel bad for wondering such a thing—what kind of mother would ever be able to return to normal living?

At this point, he wasn't shooting for normal anymore. He would settle for many things much less than normal. Somewhere between there and his current crisis would be acceptable.

His children were his joy. The oldest four had already left home, but he still had the younger three—and David, of course. Oscar missed the days when he had been able to spend more time playing with them. He always felt better about them when he was around. He felt bad leaving Leron to care for them on her own so often, but he didn't know what else to do. Cotton called. Oscar felt especially bad because there had been plenty of times with the older children when Leron had answered cotton's call herself, pulling her babies behind her on tow sacks as she slaved away in the hot sun.

Even Oscar's steep work ethic wasn't enough to provide—and it ate away at Leron. He could tell.

And then there was Loretta, youngest of their older set of children. She was a fourteen-year-old firecracker, but at least she could help with Willard and Judy—and especially the new baby, David. Oscar knew David wouldn't be small enough to cradle for long. There was a life coming for him. A world that would not understand or accept him. And a host of bills that would trail behind him.

No one wants to think of their own children in this way, but it must be done. Reality makes demands. And Oscar was out of strength. Out of courage. Out of money.

Back at the house that Sunday afternoon, the popping and crackling of thin bologna strips frying in an iron skillet filled their air with a familiar sweet aroma. But it was still bologna. Oscar hung his suit coat as neatly as he could in the small closet and slipped into his work trousers. He only had one suit, but he had four pairs of work pants. Even the clothes were screaming at him about who he was meant to be . . . and who he would never be.

There was still a lot of daylight left, and as much as he wanted to honor the Sabbath day, the odor of cheap luncheon meat was all he had smelled for months. The ends were not meeting, so after dinner he would go to the field waiting for his labor.

He walked into the small kitchen. Leron was at the stove, where she always was. Loretta was tending to the new baby and the other kids were—well, being kids.

"Children! Come to the table right now!"

Leron's voice seemed to do the trick. The whole family gathered for their meal, modest though it may be. Bologna, with its edges cut away so it wouldn't shrivel up in the skillet. Mashed potatoes. Pickled okra from a jar that resided in the small pantry closet with ten other jars given to the Rings by Sister Ethel last fall.

What would they do without the charity in those jars? It would be nice if some of them contained Joshua's milk and honey from Oscar's sermon, but beggars could not be choosers. And that's close to what they were.

Oscar croaked out a small blessing and the family began to eat.

"That was a good sermon this morning, honey." Leron's voice was sweet and gentle.

Oscar was normally a kind, compassionate man. He loved his family and was affectionate toward each of them. But today he was consumed by the dryness. The yearning. He continued to look at the floor.

"Thanks."

"Are you going to rest this afternoon?"

"Can't."

The one-word answers troubled Leron, but she didn't want to poke at the hornets' nest. Not again. Not in front of the kids. She resigned herself to the fact that a quiet lunch was better than a loud one.

Suddenly a blood-curdling cry came from the crib in the corner. It was sudden and unnerving, making everyone at the table jump. Oscar dropped his fork and it banged loudly on his plate, which only seemed to send the baby into greater hysterics.

"Can't you do something about that baby?" He put his elbows on the table and ran his fingers through his brown hair. It was beginning to become peppered with white highlights.

Leron had the baby in her arms in a matter of seconds, but the screaming continued. It was different from the cries of her other babies when they had been so little. More raw.

"There, there, my little miracle. Momma's got you. Shhh." The screaming suddenly ceased as the baby's mouth found what it really needed—food.

Leron looked up at Oscar to find him still bent over the table, seeming to be in agony. The sight of it got the best of her. "He's your baby too, you know," she said. "Maybe you should just calm down a little bit. He's just hungry."

"We're all hungry!" Oscar yelled. "We've been eating this God-forsaken dog-meat for months now! It would be nice if just for one moment we could eat it in peace and quiet!"

The children stiffened in their chairs. Some stared at their momma. Some at their daddy. Some stared at their plates. They didn't know who would throw the next verbal punch.

But they knew better than to interrupt an argument. That would land them the job of breaking a switch off of the crape myrtle in the back.

The argument was another rapid summer storm, passing over as quickly as it had appeared. Oscar's face revealed that he hated the man he was at that moment, but his situation enslaved him. He stood up, letting his chair topple over behind him, banging hard on the wooden floor. He grabbed his boots that were lying against the wall and carried them with him as he slammed out the back door. The loud noises made the baby start crying again, and Leron started to soothe him again.

"Shhh, hush, baby. It's okay. Daddy don't mean it, sugar. Daddy don't mean nothing by it."

She brushed away a tear from her eye before it became visible to the older children. The baby grew calm at the tone of her voice—and his calmness made her calm as well. With all that was unknown and out of sorts, a little moment with her little child made her right as rain.

Before she could finish feeding him, she heard the sound of Oscar's truck starting and pulling out of the driveway. She continued softly talking to the baby. "You hear that? That's your daddy going to work—for you. For us. He don't mean to be so ornery. He's trying so hard." She looked off into the distance and continued to rock little David Ring.

Not enough food. Not enough money. Not enough of anything in this place but cotton. If you could bake cotton into a casserole, that would change everything.

The baby finally settled into a peaceful sleep, so she laid him in on the bed in her bedroom and went back to work washing the dishes. He couldn't roll over by himself, so she knew he would be safe.

As she was clearing the table, she came to Oscar's plate, still full, and carefully scraped every bit of food into a napkin. Nothing could be discarded in the life of a preacher's family.

She wouldn't say what she was thinking somewhere deep inside. Somewhere in a back room, quarantined by her faith. Somewhere in the blackest closet beneath one of the floorboards was a thought she never wanted to unearth. Yet she knew it was there and hated its presence, for it was a thought she had given birth to as surely as she had given birth to her little ones. And it was an unhealthy thought.

Where is God in all of this?

Had she said it out loud, or only let it out of its closet in her mind for a split second? She couldn't tell. She was that lost in thought—moving unconsciously from task to task in her little piece of Arkansas, a piece she didn't actually own. It owned her instead, asserting its dominance with monthly bills that couldn't be paid.

Leron didn't like this frame of mind. It never helped anything, especially not her marriage. She knew they were in trouble, so it was best to lock away the thoughts and let her hands take the lead. Work. Work some more. Surely things would change. Surely there would be an upswing.

Thus ran her thoughts for what seemed like an eternity, but it was actually only a few hours. The baby was up and ready to be fed again. The other kids were lost in their adventures somewhere outside—free to run and play in a way that would be wonderful and carefree until they too would become old enough to be owned by the soil.

She had to stop thinking.

The ring of a phone broke the spell at last.

She had the baby cradled in her left arm and picked up the phone in her right. She stopped bouncing the baby and her voice took on a tone of resolution—as if she knew she was about to be called to spring into action.

"Hello?"

It was Eddie, the owner of the cotton gin. "Where's Oscar? He's late again!" Typical Eddie.

"Eddie, it's Sunday, for God's sake! You know he heads over to Jimmy Sutton's field first on Sundays. We need the extra money. He'll be there as soon as he can."

Eddie launched into his well-rehearsed rant, but Leron checked out. The sound of his raspy voice always took her back ten years to another call she had received from him, in 1945.

"Mrs. Ring? This—this is Eddie. Eddie Jones. I work with your husband." Leron could tell he was out of breath. It was almost as if she could feel the adrenaline in his voice through the phone. And it was contagious.

"Yes, Eddie. I remember you. What's the matter?"

"Ma'am, there's been an accident with your husband."

"What happened to Oscar?"

"He was out there in the field like always, and his shirt got caught in the gin." He paused, then continued, "It pulled his arm in too."

"What? His arm? Eddie, is he still alive?" The resolve in her voice revealed another stowaway that was trying to make itself known. Panic.

Another pause on the other end. "He's alive, but it ripped up his arm pretty bad, Leron. Real bad. He's lost a lot of blood. They's taking him to the hospital right now. You oughta get on down there as quick as you can."

Ten years later, every ring of the phone still threatened to bring chaos.

6

March 1970

"Dude, are you serious?"

Jeff's face was solemn. High school solemn, which meant it could change into laughing at any second. But for the moment he was pretty serious.

"I know, but just listen. We're his only friends, understand?" I tried not to sound like my father. I could tell it wasn't working.

Tim piped in. "Not true. What about Bill Shiffle and his band of merry losers? They sure seem pretty chummy with him."

Tim was right. And we couldn't stand Bill Shiffle.

Ring had started hanging out pretty regularly with a certain group of guys, of whom Bill Shiffle was the leader. These were not the most popular kids in the school, to put it mildly. Now, all this would have been fine if they'd really sought

Ring's friendship. But anyone could see what was happening. Their main goal in life was to get Ring to do crazy stuff.

He was like their puppet—and he didn't seem to realize that when they taunted him to say or do something rude, they weren't laughing with him.

It was easy for me to see why Ring was drawn to Bill. Bill had polio and walked with a considerable limp and a leg brace. They had a connection based on their immobility. But it seemed to me that Bill didn't want or need that kind of connection. He was just eager to exploit Ring's trust.

As for Ring, he had been as cold to people in general as he'd been at first to me. But when Bill and his band of teenage buddies took him in, he became completely unbearable.

Ring had not particularly encouraged my attempts to be his friend, but somehow I still felt protective of him. I may not have even liked him all that much at the time, but I had been in his home. I had seen and thought a little about what his world was like. And I didn't want him to be used and laughed at.

But Ring didn't get it. He seemed to think that since he and Shiffle both walked with limps, they had a true bond. My fear was that if he kept hanging out with those guys, it would actually become one—and he'd become as much of a jerk as Shiffle.

"The last time we were at a baseball game," Tim pointed out, "Ring acted like a complete idiot."

I remembered what he was talking about. Ring sat in the stands that ran down the first baseline, and we sat behind home plate. I could barely concentrate on the game. They kept daring Ring to say stupid things to girls or to heckle the players—and he came through for them every time. When they laughed, he laughed too. I didn't.

Ring looked like a complete fool to everyone, and I hated it.

"Guys! What's the big deal?" I said, giving it my best try. "We're going to be sitting in the bleachers watching the game. He can sit with us, you dorks." I didn't care for baseball as much as basketball. The games took so long to play that watching it was an endurance sport itself. By the time the pitcher adjusted his cap for the seventh time in the last five minutes, spat a small moat around the pitcher's mound, called off three signals from the catcher, and decided to actually throw the ball, I could walk to the concession stand and buy a hotdog. And all that for a "Ball one!"

"Jeff, what if we bring my sister Kathy along too?" I suggested. "Would that sway your decision at all?" Jeff turned his head to the side and furrowed his brow.

"Not cool, man. Not cool at all."

Tim jumped right in with me. "Was it not cool when you held hands with her at the hayride last fall?"

Aggravation was afoot—and we were the smelly sneakers. A collective smile bounced back and forth between Tim's face and mine. Jeff's face, on the other hand, was unsuccessfully trying to hold its ground against the aggression of slight red circles developing just above his cheekbones.

"We're just friends! I don't like her, you know, that way!" Jeff protested.

"Sure you don't. You probably like her mom instead!" Tim said.

My smile quickly morphed into a hard punch in Tim's arm. "Hey! That's my mom you're talking about! When I'm out on a date with your mom, she hates it when people talk about my mom."

Tim punched me back and we all started laughing. The great thing about "mom jokes" was that they didn't have to make any sense at all. They were always funny, even when they weren't.

Tim stopped laughing and spoke with the serious tone only he could muster at such a young age. I guess it came from all his leadership roles. He was the quarterback of the football team. He was the starting point guard on the basketball team. He was the president of the junior class. He knew what it meant to guide a conversation on a forced march in a new direction.

"Look, Dave, we've all tried this before. Heck, you've tried this a hundred times since the kid moved here. We're all sorry that he has so many 'issues.'"

He put up a few air quotes as he said it. It offended me more than I thought it should. He continued. "But the dude does not want to be friends with us. And quite honestly, I'm over trying to be friends with him too. I got enough people who do want to hang out to waste my time with some retard who doesn't want to hang out."

"Tim! Shut up, moron. Too far." Jeff just shook his head in disgust. "You're an idiot sometimes."

"You know what," I said with the obvious steam of an engine about to blow a gasket, "you do what you got to do, pretty boy. I'm sorry that you've got such a reputation to guard."

Tim leaned his head to one side and glared hard at me. "You know that's not it, Dave. This is not about me thinking I'm too popular or something. This is about Ring being as stubborn as a mule every time we try to be nice to him."

I honestly couldn't argue too much with that. Ring had been pretty rude to all of us, although he would at least tolerate me, apparently since I'd paid some unspecified kind of dues. I'd made that house call the fall before, and because of that, he would speak to me in spurts. In the hall. At lunch. In class when we were supposed to be listening to the teacher.

Truthfully, those days were difficult times because as long as it was just the two of us, things were pretty endurable. But the moment a new player was introduced into the social experiment, it all went up in smoke.

My parents were consistent in urging me to be a friend to Ring. Not that I really needed that much motivation. Something inside of me wanted to be his friend—enough so that now I would fight for his cause in my most important group of friends.

I looked at Tim and calmly said, "Okay, you're right. He can be an idiot, but the guy has cerebral palsy and his mom died last year."

Tim piped in, "Yeah, okay. Last year. How long is he going to drag his cross around? It's time to move on—I mean, at least try not to be a jerk."

"Seriously?" I asked. "Your mom dying is not just something you 'get over' in a day or two."

Tim wasn't trying to be insensitive. He was only verbalizing what so many people thought about those who have faced significant losses. *Just get over it already! Your pain is inconvenient. It's awkward for the rest of us, so we're going to ask you to move on, my friend, okay?*

I had seen it a million times with my dad's stuff as a pastor. Uncle Bob just won't move past his wife's death. Aunt Sarah is wallowing in her grief. Can you talk to her, tell her to act normal?

Plus, Ring's situation was far from normal.

"Look, I don't know if he's trying or not. I do know it's one lousy baseball game. What do you say, guys? Are we man enough?"

Tim had been leaning forward in his chair and he sat all the way back to let out a long, drawn-out sigh. "Fine, Davey, if it means so much to you. But you're buying the hotdogs."

He knew I hated it when he called me Davey. I absolutely hated it. But I wore a smile as we left the cafeteria and headed for class.

The day dragged along until the bell rang to end fifth period. As usual, within five seconds a deluge of adolescent humanity flooded the hallway—students in every size, shape, and attitude all crammed into the tight area around the lockers. They moved like a pack of wildebeest, with one straggler in the rear.

Ring knew his way around that jungle of Liberty High School by now. I'd expected the football players to make fun of him, but oddly there was less of that than I'd predicted. Perhaps it was because he was so skilled at keeping to himself. He learned to wait until the masses had moved through before dragging himself to his locker.

In fact, it was the teachers who seemed most annoyed by his presence. He was always late to class, and rarely lifted a finger to do anything once he got there. But there was more to it than this. When he was called upon in class to answer a question, he could always be counted upon to drop some line of cold condescension. He had honed abrasiveness to a fine art.

In English class, Mrs. Godwin asked him if he had his homework. To which Ring replied, "No, I ate it."

"Do you mean your dog ate it?" Mrs. Godwin replied in a gentle tone. Middle-aged with hair just turning gray, she was a little portly and a little self-conscious of it. But she was a kind person. She wanted to go easy on the special needs kid.

Ring looked back at Bill Shiffle, who nodded with a smirk. Ring fired back without hesitation. "No, I mean I ate it befoh yuh wouwd have a chance to eat it."

The whole class erupted into laughter, and Mrs. Godwin's face turned the deep hue of embarrassment.

But Ring knew he had the upper hand. No way would she send him to detention. You had to go easy on the "disadvantaged" kids. Heck, even writing penalties seemed like cruel punishment for a kid who had so much trouble with pencils and paper. Thankfully for Ring, the bell rung before Mrs. Godwin had time to process what to do. He was saved by the bell and the questionable perks of cerebral palsy.

Mrs. Godwin was not the only faculty victim of Ring's rudeness. Rumors of his sour demeanor, especially in the face of kindness and patience, had spread throughout the entire teaching staff. How did I know this? Teachers live under the mistaken belief that kids lose their power of hearing and perception as long as adults are talking to other adults and they are ten or fifteen feet away.

The other day I had overheard Coach Hall and Mrs. Flagmere talking at the door after gym class just before the bell was supposed to ring. I was lucky enough to have gym the last period of the day, which meant Coach Hall would usually get pretty lax about how many push-ups and sit-ups we had to do. He would opt for dodgeball instead—meaning he got to play too. He had a killer arm, and it gave him joy to hurl the ball at freshmen and sophomores diving for cover. It was like coaching therapy.

The game was over and we were nursing our bruises and putting our sweaty clothes back in our gym lockers. I finished changing and stood by the gym door, hoping to catch a little bit of the cool breeze that blew through every time someone entered or exited.

Coach Hall leaned back against the wall, spinning his whistle in circles. "He did what? I don't believe it."

"I'm not lying, Bill! That kid called me an ugly cow in front of my whole class! I couldn't believe it either. I've got a pretty good idea Bill Shiffle and his crew dared him to do it. They were giggling, thick as thieves, at the whole thing. I was mortified!"

"And what did Principal Davenport say about it?"

"That's the craziest part! He told me that David Ring was a special case and that he would talk to him about it. Any other kid? He would have sent him to detention for a week!"

Coach Hall adjusted his polyester shorts. "If you ask me, that kid needs to be in a special school."

"I know," said an exasperated Mrs. Flagmere. "But they say he does well enough on all the standardized tests to be in regular school."

Coach Hall began popping his knuckles one by one. "What that boy needs is a good butt-kicking out on the football field."

"Bill, you know he couldn't cut it out there. Those boys would kill him. He's a sad case, even if he is one of the most annoying students I've ever had in class." The two of them went on talking, changing the subject to some other objectionable student.

This was the kind of reputation Ring was making with the adults in our school, especially the women. I was still trying to build whatever peculiar friendship we had, but it felt like Noah building the ark all by himself. Ring was not lifting a finger to help, and I was running out of patience. I was getting tired of being a one-kid crusade. My friends were getting tired of me getting tired of it. Worst of all, Ring wouldn't do a thing to help himself.

I found him at his locker awkwardly trying to put an English textbook back in so he could grab his geography book. It seemed like his fingers were having a harder time than usual finding the dexterity to make things work.

"Hey, Ring." His eyes moved my direction, but he said nothing. Typical Ring. I persisted, turning up the volume a bit. "I said, 'Hey, Ring.'"

Nothing but heavy breathing and the continuation of his fumbling through books and random papers. I decided to let it go.

"Me and Tim and Jeff thought you might want to come hang out at the baseball game this afternoon. It starts about 4:00. You in?"

"I hayt base . . . baw."

I was over it. "Fine, Ring! You sit around here hating everything—I'm done."

And I smacked the locker next to him. It made a clanging echo down the long hallway disproportionately louder than my actual smack, and I was glad. He jumped a little bit, and broke his self-imposed sight embargo to look at me. His eyes were not angry. They were concerned.

This just ticked me off even more. I'd heard this song before and I knew that he would extend just enough civility to keep me on the hook.

I just couldn't understand why it had to be such a mystery with him. Was it so incredibly hard simply to stop acting like a jerk? A couple of million things in my life, his life, and the school around us would be better for it.

"Save it!" I barked, and walked past him. I didn't mean to, but I accidentally bumped him as I passed and he dropped the geography book on the tile floor. A dozen scrap sheets of notebook paper spilled out of the book. Our little private skirmish now looked like a full-out battle—and it also looked, for all the world, as if I had knocked his book out of his hands on purpose.

The typical onlookers gathered around us. A few giggling freshman girls. One or two gawkers. And a few football players who seemed a little too amused. I did not like it—not one bit. Just then a teacher walked up on the scene. Now I was liking this whole scenario even less.

It was Ms. Myers, the psychology teacher. She was younger than most of the faculty. Prettier too. She had soft blonde hair that hung just low enough to kiss the top of her shoulders. She was one of those rare teachers you could tell was a real human being; that is, you could imagine her having an actual life outside the campus. It didn't hurt that you could also actually tell she was a woman by the way her clothes accented her curves just so.

"David? Are you okay?"

"Yes, ma'am," I replied sheepishly.

"I wasn't talking to you." She didn't yell it, but her tone was gruff enough to rattle my stomach a bit. Ring didn't say a word—typical. He knew what had really happened, but now I was going to look like the bully.

"Ms. Myers, I promise it's not what it looks like. You see, I—"

"You mean you did not knock Mr. Ring's books out of his hands? And now you are not standing here watching rather than helping to pick them up, as all these lovely people pass by?"

I was becoming more speechless with each word she spoke. These were uncharted waters for me—and I was drowning in them. Hey, I was the preacher's kid!

I could feel my gaze suddenly nosedive to the floor. I scanned the swirling designs in the tile—and the more-than-occasional blot of old chewing gum now turned black and hidden as a permanent part of the floor. I felt about like one of those blots.

"Mr. Wideman, I expect so much more from you. I wonder what your father would have to say about this?"

"Ma'am, if you would just listen to me, I promise it is not what you think."

"You can save it for Principal Davenport. Come on, let's go."

I took a deep breath and began walking with her toward the main office. I just knew that certain death awaited me at home—and for nothing but trying to invite Ring to a baseball game. I vowed that mistake as my last one regarding David Ring.

"Wayeet." It was the same "wait" I had heard in his basement a few months back. "Dayvid didden do anythang wong. It was an acciden'."

Ms. Myers looked at me suspiciously, as if I was orchestrating this whole thing. I just raised my eyebrows, clearly signaling, *What? I'm just standing here.*

"David, I saw him knock those books out of your hand. Don't defend him. You didn't do anything wrong here."

She spoke to Ring with the kindness I had tried to speak to him with for so long. It was the first time I had heard a female successfully do so—without some smart-aleck retort.

Ring looked her in the eyes. "No, ma'am. Dayvid didden mean to do it. He's my fwiend." I was as shocked as she was to hear him say it. He kept his eyes locked on Ms. Myers. In the world of teenage boys, it would not suffice to actually look at the guy you were helping out. I just stood there watching the whole thing as if I was not a participant in it.

Ms. Myers turned to me and said, "Well, I guess you're off the hook, Mr. Wideman. If David here is such a great friend, maybe you should start showing it by picking up that book and those papers so mysteriously scattered on the floor."

She walked away and there we were again—Ring and me. What was I supposed to say now? Thanks? That would indicate that I had actually done something wrong and needed rescue. It still seemed to me that the whole mess would never have transpired if he'd just been a decent guy and said yes to the baseball game.

But the incident gave me another glimpse of what was inside Ring—the real Ring. Beyond the limp, the slurred words, and the hard shell compensating for them—inside all of that, there was a real person. So yes, I said thanks, and I told myself it was more of a peace offering than any earned gratitude.

"Yo' welcome."

The bell rang just after he said it and we went off to class. During sixth period, I brooded over what it all meant. Later that afternoon, I watched for him at the baseball game.

He never showed.

7

That Same Afternoon

Loretta drapes her purse over her arm and opens the front door so her kids can run past. “The doctor’s appointment shouldn’t take more than a few hours. We’ll be back in time for dinner, okay?”

“Okay, girl! You guys be careful!” Debbie says.

“And David, don’t forget. Debbie is in charge while I’m gone. You do whatever she says, you hear?” She doesn’t wait for his reply and the door slams shut. Soon the sound of the car engine fades down the street and David is standing alone in the living room with Debbie.

“I’m goin’ to the basebaw game.”

Debbie’s face quickly finds a new expression. She is sassy. Playful. With one hand on her hip. “Baseball game? Why would you want to go to some baseball game? You don’t even like baseball.”

David stands sullen and silent, with his eyes on the floor.

"Dayvid invited meh."

"I don't think so."

She turns to the right and gazes hard out the front double windows of the house. Then her eyes move back to David, and a faint smile comes across her face. David feels his stomach twist.

"Rod won't be home for another hour, and the kids are at the doctor." She has moved closer to him, and now she casually drops a hand toward his knee.

He takes hold of that hand and tosses it violently away from himself.

"No!" David roars, as much as it is possible for someone like him to roar. "No more! I'm not doin' dis agin!"

Tears of rage and despair fill his eyes. And one other thing, the worst of things. Shame. He lurches toward the hook where his jacket hangs, grabs the coat, and focuses every muscle, every ability, on getting to the door.

Now a new tone comes from Debbie—one of cold authority. "David. You get back here right now. Or you know what will happen."

David halts with the doorknob in his hand and hangs his head, but will not face her. Outside the sun is shining. He hears the laughter of children down the street.

"Look," she says, "I've already told you. This is what your momma would want. For all of us to stay close after she died. We're all you've got left. Where on the face of this earth could you go, David, but here?"

Her voice has become gentler as she subtly moves toward him. She grabs his shoulder with one hand and pushes the door closed with the other. "Besides," she says in a little-girl kind of way that revolts him, "don't you think I'm pretty?"

"Yo' my sistuh's best fwiend," he mutters, beaten down, knowing the words that should mean everything will mean nothing in helping him.

"It doesn't matter, David. What matters is that you do what your momma wants you to do and don't tell nobody. You know I don't have no choice but to be here. You think I want to be here living with you? You don't know what it's like to get married and get the daylights beat out of you every time they run a happy hour down at The Waterin' Hole. You don't care about me! No one does!"

She escalates into dramatic hysterics with each word before emotionally collapsing into a heap of sobbing. As she recovers herself, she leans in closely, and her bottom lip grazes his ear as she whispers, "Look, just because Dan doesn't love me doesn't mean you can't. Besides, I'd hate to have to tell Loretta what you've done. Why, she'd send you off to the crazy house, where you'd be all alone. They'd tie you up like an animal. Treat you like a retard. Is that what you want, David?"

Her voice is direct and unyielding. Authoritative.

The tears are now streaming down David's cheek, though he's unaware of them. He shakes his head no, but still he averts his eyes. Always, he averts his eyes, and in his mind he goes to some dark, solitary place. It's all he can do.

She takes him by the hand and leads him to her room. "Just this one more time, David? For your Debbie? I promise. It won't hurt anything."

They disappear into the bedroom, and the door clicks shut.

8

April 1970

"You okay, Wideman?"

I lay on the field in a heap. It was the first time I had ever just "eaten it" at a track practice. Coach Hall made all the basketball players run track simply to keep us in good shape during the off-season. Otherwise, you couldn't have paid me to be on the track team.

I did manage to avoid some of the running by signing up for the long jump and shot put. But today the joke was on me. Coach had made us warm up by doing a few sprints in the middle field of the track. I had lost my footing when I lunged to touch the ground and turn to sprint back. The result was a very ungraceful face plant in the grass—and a whole lot of laughing from the rest of the guys on the team.

There would have been a hole in the ground the shape of my nose if the ground hadn't been so hard. So the ground won that battle. April showers had not come our way, and it was the hottest April anyone could remember. Dry too. Crispy dry. The ground was like hardtack. Probably as tasty too, though I hadn't been around during the Civil War to become an expert on that. I stood up and spit out the white, dead Bermuda and jogged back to the line to join the rest of the guys who were warming up.

I really didn't care for track practice, but I didn't mind the early heat. It reminded me of being in the hot gym during summer basketball camp. There was something about the blistering heat. The sheets of sweat pouring down and stinging your eyes. That shiver you feel up and down your spine when you know you are too hot—way too hot. Even though it was a sign you were not too far from heat exhaustion, I had a strange love for that feeling.

I also loved pick-up games outside on the city courts in the summer. The blinding sun. The occasional breeze that blew in from the south—like an electric hair dryer on high, but still somehow refreshing. Most people complained about the conditions, but I always loved it. I'm not sure why.

It was a long practice, and the pungent stench of the locker room proved it. Sneakers and jock straps were strewn all over the floor, some draped on the wooden benches and some hanging down from the tops of the lockers.

There are some youthful fragrances you don't wish to revisit.

Jeff's hair was still wet from his shower, and it spiked from his head. But he had already started sweating again through his shirt. He had pinched a bit of his cotton fabric between his thumb and forefinger and was quickly pulling it back and forth from his chest, creating a makeshift fanning system. His shower didn't take.

"Dude! It's burning up—can we please go before I have to take another shower?"

I put my shoes into my locker and stuffed my track uniform into my gym bag. I didn't take it home to wash after every practice, but it had been five days and Mom would give me an earful if she had to open my bag to find that kind of surprise again.

"I'm ready. Let's do it." We emerged from the locker room and walked through the school parking lot, turning at the end onto the sidewalk to head toward my house. We talked the usual stuff. Who was going to start at point guard next season. Who was going to beat those evil Pittsburgh Steelers come autumn. What lucky and no-doubt jerkish frat boy was going to date Summer Havenstead next year. Lucky jerkish frat boy. We reached my house in about fifteen minutes and came through the front door to see Mom in the kitchen.

"Hey boys! David, stop right there and leave that bag on the porch. I'll not have you stinking up the house right before dinner." I looked at Jeff and rolled my eyes.

"I saw that!" No way she could have seen the eye-roll. I think mothers are just perfect students of human behavior. She knew me so well that she anticipated my reactions. And she was almost always right.

We settled in around the table. Dad took his position at the end near the china cabinet, while Mom sat directly across from him at the other end. Their seats were as established as the polar ice caps. Meat loaf and mashed potatoes were piled high in the middle of the table, steaming into the air and making my mouth water. I was usually starved after practice, and today was no exception.

Kathy sat to my right and Jeff took the seat right across from her. They did not look at each other or speak to each other—not in front of Mom and Dad. Not because my parents would not approve, but just because. It was a collision of worlds no teenager was comfortable with.

But we were a very close family, and my parents talked to us about everything. They knew what was going on between Kathy and Jeff, pulling it out of her like an embedded wisdom tooth. Kathy usually felt better when things like that were finally out, but oh, how she resisted the tugging.

Mom and Dad loved every minute of it—being part of our lives was what they lived for. Their love was evident, even when an extraction was necessary. It would be years before I could fully appreciate the value of their gift. But tonight they were being good and giving Jeff and Kathy a free pass to eat dinner with minimal embarrassment.

"Kathy, would you please ask the blessing?" Dad looked at her with a little smile. She was by no means ashamed to pray, but everything changes when there is a boy at the house—even if it is your brother's best friend.

"Yessir." She bowed her head and quietly cleared her throat. "Our heavenly Father, thank you for this food we are about to eat. Please bless it and the hands that have prepared it. Amen."

In our house, the word *amen* was more than the stereotypical end of a prayer. It was the flag that started the horses galloping.

The table erupted with a new energy as dishes and spoons began clanging in the process of self-plating. It was a good sound tied to good memories. It felt like the essence of family. As the sun cascaded through the dining room window, illuminating those tiny particles of dust that I guess are always floating in the air, I felt full. And I had yet to even take a bite of food.

I remedied that quickly.

The conversation was typical. Polite yet personal. What classes we were planning to take next fall. Our upcoming match-up with Fort Osage High, our district rivals. How Jeff's parents were coming along at work. Jeff always felt like family, answering questions with cheeks bulging with food, so it was always fun to have him with us.

Dad stood to walk into the kitchen, returning in a moment with a pitcher of sweet tea. "Anyone need a refill?" Kathy and Mom were fine with their glasses, but Jeff and I were parched. Refills abounded and Dad sat back down, taking a lemon wedge from a little plate on the table and squeezing it into his tea, then stirring it a bit with the tip of his finger. Mom just gave him a look.

"What? They're my germs," he said. He took a quick drink and then picked up his fork again. "Boys, have you heard anything from David Ring lately?"

What could we say? Truth was, any small hope of actually becoming real friends with Ring had faded away months ago. We had invited him, mostly unsuccessfully, to dozens of events. Games. Stuff with my youth group. Even over to the house for dinner with my folks—an honor in which all of my friends indulged themselves. Mom's meat loaf was the stuff of legend.

Occasionally Ring would reluctantly agree and tag along, but it would always end badly. He would play the recluse in the corner. Ignore people who were addressing him. Or when he did speak, it was always something sarcastic or rude.

Many people at our school had tried to treat him well, to give him some kind of place in the social order, but he'd been such a jerk to so many of them that the tide had turned, and people figured he deserved whatever consequences he got.

Soon dislike turned into ridicule, as they imitated his drawl and his movements.

I tried to look the other way, but the number of David Ring impressionists continued to grow rapidly. They had the walk down. The speech impediment. If I were being honest, this kid named Sid at school had him pegged so perfectly that one day I was horrified to find myself chuckling under my breath. It was not intentional, and I quickly pulled it together. On the other hand, a little voice inside me insisted that Ring kind of had it coming.

Now, at the family table, I made furrows in my mashed potatoes with my fork as Dad waited for the answer to his question. It was my third helping, so I figured it could wait. I avoided eye contact.

"Ring does not want to hang out, Dad. I've tried. I really have."

Jeff had my flank. "He's right, Brother Don. I promise we have tried a hundred times. The guy is just kind of—well, rude." He quickly took a drink after he said it, obviously uncomfortable over the perception that he was judging Ring because of his disability. It was just hard to say that a guy with cerebral palsy was not a very likable person. The time-honored idea was that some people were injured by the side of the road, and we were the Good Samaritans.

But being "injured" was no excuse for being a jerk. At least that's how it seemed up to that point.

We waited for the rebuke, but it never came. Dad simply stared at his tea, making marks in the foggy condensation on the glass. He sat there for at least two minutes—so long, in fact, that we all just went back to eating, figuring he must have drifted off mentally. Then he spoke out of the blue.

"You know, boys, people are like tea."

Jeff and I exchanged glances. Dad was a preacher, so the analogies were plentiful in our house. He was always there to make sure we saw the forest and not just the trees. It was like living with a forest ranger of everyday ethics.

Which was fine with me. I loved hearing what Dad might say, and as much as I hated to admit it, it usually was something profound and helpful.

I was the first one to nibble at the bait he was dangling out there. "How so, Pops?"

He never looked up. He remained fixated on the glass before him. "Tea doesn't just appear. It is made through a process of steeping. First of all, the water must be boiling hot. Heat changes things, whether they want to change or not. The bubbles rise, and the steam heats the air. Anything that goes into that water is going to come out different."

The entire dinner table was now staring at his glass too. He had us, and he knew it.

"Then a tea bag is dropped into the boiling water—like I said, it immediately begins to change. All that is dry and compact begins to seep out of the bag and liquefy. At first, you can even see a brown cloud begin to expand throughout the water—like the winding boundary of two territories: water and tea. They are separate."

He then picked up the glass. "But the longer that bag is in that water, the more the two borders disappear into each other. The brown takes over, and if you wait long enough, the water is no longer water. Now the whole pot is filled with nothing but tea."

We were mulling that one over when he turned to me. "David, people are like tea. When they are thrown into hot water—whether of their own doing or not—they are changed by their circumstances. How can they not be? And the longer they stay in the heat, the more they become one with their difficulty. It begins to define them. Pretty soon they are just tea. They are just bitter. They are just depressed. They are just angry. They become steeped in their situation. Lost in it until it consumes them."

Then he gazed out the window and let the idea brew within us. He drew a long breath and said, "Only God can cool the heat—separate the tea back from the water. Sometimes he even puts other people near the heat. People who can endure it. People equipped to help that person regain hope again."

It all sounded very nice. You had to be impressed with someone who could look at a glass of sweet tea and define the problems of the world through it. And I knew in my heart that every word Dad said was true, and that it probably defined David's issues with precision. But I had given my best effort. I'd done my thing, and that was more than nearly anyone else had done. I had been rejected. If Ring didn't want to be my friend, then I wasn't going to force it on him.

For the moment, I did have a good friend handy. His name was Jeff, and we had plans for that evening. It was a nice night, and we were going to set out for Kuku, the burger joint where our buddies around town hung out. We were ready to have some fun—and wasn't that what friendship was all about?

9

June 1959

"Don't send me away, Leron. I'm begging you! For the children!"

"Oscar, it's over. You need to leave."

Oscar didn't want to leave. Even with everything he knew. Even with all the grievances any husband would have, he wanted to tough it all out. Because that's how you did things in this kind of life.

But Leron could see no way forward but separate paths. So with a sigh of resignation, Oscar continued to use his one good arm to throw all the clothes he owned into a large, battered suitcase.

For Leron, the decision had been made long since. She could never take back what she had done, and the damage was what it was. There could be no more together for Oscar and

Leron. The affair had not been a thing she had planned—it was just something that happened. Like every disaster in life.

"I guess a one-armed man just wasn't enough for you, was it?" he asked bitterly. "In some ways, I guess I can see that. But some kid? You've got to be kidding me!"

J. D. was years younger than Leron—about the age of her oldest son, Gilbert. The affair had been going on for quite some time. Who knows what brought the distance between Oscar and Leron that let J. D. find a place between them—the cotton gin accident? The poverty? The children? Regardless, the chasm was there; it was wide and it was deep.

Leron's mind was made up, and such things only required one vote. She would no longer accept Oscar's presence. He was more than devastated by this turn of events. He still loved her. He adored his precious children, and he was willing to try, but Leron's heart had calcified. The marriage had been over for a long time on her personal timeline. She felt she needed a clean break, or else she knew the guilt and pain of what was happening might decimate her.

She heard the old door crunch shut, and for the final time those familiar footsteps trudged toward the truck. Inside the small house, Leron felt the unpleasant tingle of aloneness. But it wasn't going to last. J. D. was the answer. He would fill the emotional hole inside her. She just knew it.

"Momma!" The little six-year-old boy awkwardly moved into the living room. Against all odds, he had never crawled but went straight to walking. Leron figured the abrupt slam of the door must have awakened the boy from his nap. As always, she felt a tinge of both joy and sadness as she took in his struggling figure.

Whatever she was feeling, it wasn't catching. The boy's eyes lit up at the sight of his mother and a wide smile lightened his features. She turned toward him as he lifted his little arms to signal he wanted to be held. "Momma!"

She closed her eyes and wrapped him in a tight embrace. "Baby, Momma isn't such a good momma right now," she murmured.

Her own words took her aback. Something about this child brought things out of her that she didn't know were there. He wrapped his arms around her neck and squeezed with all the strength his little body could muster. He had no idea what she'd said or done. He loved his momma. He laid his head on her shoulder and closed his eyes.

Leron looked out the window at the cloud of brown exhaust from Oscar's old truck. She leaned her head against David's and rocked him back and forth.

Her tough exterior was now transformed into tenderness. "Momma's got you, my angel. That's who you are—my angel."

Within a matter of a few weeks, Leron took David and his sister Judy—who was two years older than he was—and moved them out into the boonies to the little town of Brookland, Arkansas. Leron and J. D. bought the house together. He brought along his three kids from a previous marriage, so the newly mixed family was a busy one.

David was very young, but he understood that J. D. was not his daddy and he was never really easy around the new man of the house. The divorce was never talked about. It would be years before little David would piece things together and begin to understand. In the meantime, he lived in a simple cosmos whose center was Momma. The man didn't seem to fit into it, but everything was all right as long as she was in place.

Three years later, the phone call came. Leron was holding the phone, hearing the words that came across the line—and a coffee mug fell from her grasp, smashing into jagged pieces on the green linoleum floor. "When?" she said quietly. "Okay. I understand. Thanks for calling."

She hung up the receiver and sat down in one of the kitchen chairs. No tears streamed down her cheeks. No tears, that is, until the little boy hobbled into the room. "Momma, yuh okeh?"

She pulled the little boy close to her and gently stroked his light brown hair. "Baby, I don't know how to tell you this, but it's your daddy—"

"Daddy's comin' home, Momma?"

Now the tears overtook her. "No, angel. Your daddy got sick with something they call the cancer. He just went to heaven, baby."

He had never really known his father; Leron hadn't permitted it. Old chapters in a book cannot be revised. Old failures must be put behind. What David would later discover was that, after the breakup, Oscar had fallen into a deep depression. What was there in life for him, if not his family?

Once or twice David had seen his daddy; an older brother had snuck him over to Oscar's place. But it wasn't like really having a daddy, knowing him and loving him every day. David hadn't had that, and now he never would.

The older children now rekindled their fury against their mother over the whole affair and divorce. They had screamed at her more times than she could recount, but when she chose a path she would not stray from it, nor would those in her care. The children never truly made peace with their mother's decisions, and when Oscar passed it was easy to believe he had died of a broken heart. They were so angry in their grief that they forbade Leron to even come to his funeral.

On the day of the terrible phone call, David was still a little boy. His view of life's horizons was very limited. But somehow he understood he had lost something precious, something essential. Perhaps he could read it in the regret-filled eyes of his mother. A great, gaping hole was there in a place where there should be fullness and joy.

He had no daddy. He never would have one. Little David buried his head against his momma's bosom and cried softly as she rocked him back and forth. He had sorrow, but no bitterness. How could he? His mother was his world, his one irreplaceable thing.

At least, he knew with a child's faith, he would always have her.

10

April 1970

After dinner, Jeff and I set out for Kuku in town. Kuku was a little hamburger joint where we would all go after basketball games and the like. They sold burgers for nineteen cents. It was the place where the whole school would come to hang out, it seemed. Honestly, there weren't too many other places to go—and we liked it that way.

It was the perfect gathering place for warm nights like this one. Now that we were older, it wasn't off-limits even on school nights. As Jeff and I strolled down the sidewalk, talking more about the upcoming summer, I reflected that this was a nice time and a nice place. The sky had that hue to it unique to dusk. The blue was morphing into black, but it wasn't quite there yet, and brushstrokes of pink and orange were being painted near the horizon as the sun began its descent behind the Ozarks. Life was good.

That's when I heard it. "David! You get back in this house right now!" The voice was threatening, demanding. As I looked up, it occurred to me that we were standing on Lewis Street, right in front of Ring's house. And as we tried to make sense of the voice we'd heard, the screen door slammed open and Ring himself appeared. Seeming intent and in his own world, he hobbled his way down the front steps. Jeff and I stood and stared.

"I mean it, David Ring! Come back inside or I'll tell Loretta what you done!"

And there was Debbie, the owner of the voice. She was now standing on the porch yelling, but Ring was paying no heed. He was already halfway down the driveway. I marveled at the speed he could move when he really wanted to. I suppose a person can become pretty efficient in their deficiencies if they are given enough time or enough motivation.

Debbie's hair was all messed up, like she had just rolled out of bed. And she was wearing an old pink bathrobe. As she walked out, she was in the process of tying the cotton belt around the robe.

David looked awful. His shirt was untucked and his face was redder than the subtle shades of the sunset behind us. Clearly, this was all a puzzle piece in some larger story. We weren't trying to intrude; the situation intruded on us at the spot we happened to be standing.

Debbie started down the driveway to catch Ring, but then she noticed us standing there. It seemed as if something changed for her, some intention, because of our presence. She turned, walked back inside, and shut both the screen door and the front door behind her.

As he neared the sidewalk, I spoke up. "Ring? You okay?"

I honestly don't think he knew we were standing there. He brushed past Jeff without saying a word. For once it didn't seem like rudeness, but as if his body and mind were in two different locations. He headed down the street in the opposite direction of our destination.

Jeff looked at me with the same expression I was no doubt giving him. "That was weird," he said with huge eyes. Then, as if to turn the page, he added, "Let's go."

But something kept my feet from moving. The spring evening sense of wellbeing had fled in the presence of this mystery. "I—I can't. Not tonight. I'm going to follow Ring."

Jeff's face expressed no disapproval. More like a pitied understanding. We both knew that we had just seen a guy who was definitely in some boiling water, and the borders were long gone. We also knew there was a reason we were standing on this particular patch of ground. Dad was right—again.

"You want me to go with you?" Jeff asked.

"Nah, that's okay. I was the one who got us into this Ring business."

Jeff nodded, but with a clear twinge of regret for the hang-out time we were losing together with our friends. It just wasn't meant to be—he would go on without me.

I hurried down the road after Ring, who was definitely on a mission of some kind. I was actually having trouble catching up with him. He headed toward the old sawmill down by the river. By this time the sun had finished setting. The only way I could really see him anymore was by the glow of the streetlights and the occasional passing car's headlights. His silhouette was striking—like an afflicted shadow. A tortured ghost stumbling through the darkness in search of some kind of respite. That stumbling figure, pushing through the dark, was an image I would never forget.

The old sawmill was a common rendezvous for young couples eager for a little privacy from prying parental eyes. It was also used by kids for a clandestine sip of a beer or puff of a cigarette. The place was derelict and secluded, a haven for those not wanting to be found.

But the sawmill was not Ring's destination. He continued down the left shoulder of Nashua Road. He walked for a long time, ignoring my presence behind him. We passed Lewis and Clark Elementary School and followed the road onward toward I-35. The sound of the interstate traffic grew as we drew near, especially the tractor trailers careening down the highway. By this time I was extremely curious where this moonlight expedition was heading.

Ring walked all the way across the bridge spanning the river of interstate traffic. He ran his right hand down the thick tubular railing meant to keep cars from toppling off the bridge. He looked over the side as he walked, but he never stopped. This made me feel better. But what was going on in his mind?

As soon as he had crossed the bridge, he sat down on the steel guardrail that paralleled the ramp from which cars were exiting the interstate to pull onto Highway 291. The cars were whizzing past both below us and beside us. The wind from the highway and the smell of diesel exhaust were a little stifling. It wasn't a place made for pedestrians to linger, and it all felt wrong to me.

I could see him sitting on the guardrail, but I was still about fifty yards away as I crossed the bridge, and I was thinking of what I could say to him.

But before I could get there, he stood up and walked out into the middle of the lane on the off-ramp. He didn't cross it—he stopped dead in the center, set his feet, and faced the interstate, as if some decision had been firmed up in his mind. Then he began walking as fast as he could down the ramp. Ahead of him, I could see the lights of an eighteen-wheeler exiting the interstate at a good clip. I could look at Ring and the truck and easily do the math; the truck would never have time to stop.

I didn't even think. A great flood of adrenaline coursed through my entire being, and my legs, tired though they may have been, moved into a sprint. All my resolve was compressed into one desire: to keep this insanity from occurring before my eyes.

"Ring! Get out of the road!" I didn't have much wind for screaming, since I was sprinting, but I yelled it out anyway.

Ring never flinched, never turned. Maybe he couldn't hear me. He trudged onward toward his meeting with the speeding truck, which showed no signs of slowing.

I wasn't the fastest guy on the basketball team, but I doubt anyone could have beaten me in that moment. I ran down the right side of the lane. The truck was only about twenty yards away.

"Ring!" I yelled. He turned in my direction, and I saw the most tortured, desperate face I had ever seen. "Move!"

And then I was on him, overpowering him easily. It wasn't the way you see in the movies, with me shoving him away or making a spectacular dive. I just wrapped him in a bear hug, pinning his arms to his side, and half-carried, half-dragged him to the side of the ramp.

Ring fought back. He squirmed, screaming in words I couldn't understand; you needed the best of conditions to understand him anyway. He was like a wild animal caught in a trap and giving vent to his rage.

But he would just have to go on being angry. I was stronger and I was dead set on keeping my reluctant friend alive.

The truck was a blaring, gusting blur as it rushed past us. We were in the gravel of the shoulder, and the rushing wind nearly knocked us over. I glanced up just in time to see the silhouette of a driver chugging from a coffee mug as he passed.

He'd never even seen us in the darkness.

Ring's elbow jerked my forearm. "Lemme go!" he screamed. I just increased the tightness of my hold. Tonight I'd run track, made a football tackle, and now was in a wrestling match. I'd put in quite a day.

I looked down the exit ramp and saw that no more cars were coming, so I took a good look at Ring and decided to let go. He stumbled away from me and then turned to face me. "Wha' ah yuh doin' heuh?" We were both sucking in great mouthfuls of air.

"What am I doing here? Are you crazy? You almost got us both killed! What are you doing here?"

"Yuh shoulduh wet meh awone—yuh shouldnuv fowowed meh!"

"You better be glad I did follow you, you jerk! If somebody hadn't, you'd be dead right now!"

"I wanna die!" Tears were streaming down his face. He had been moving closer to me the whole time we were shouting, so much so that he was spitting on me. Then he balled up his fist and took a swing at me. It was pathetically slow—the best one he could probably muster in such a time and place. I just took a half step back and let him miss. The momentum from his punch threw him off balance, and he went down like a sack of dirt in the gravel.

He didn't get up. He just lay there with dust and gravel on his face, sobbing. And it wasn't the kind of crying a kid does when they are hurt or upset. I'd never heard such wailing before. It was as if deep, trapped emotions were fighting their way out for the first time. A minute passed. Then two. Then five. The sobbing never lessened, not even a bit. I stood watching, catching my breath.

By this time, I was calm and rational even if he wasn't. So I sat down beside him in the gravel and watched the cars and trucks shoot by. One of them slowed down and looked hard at us, but no one stopped. We must have been a sight.

I put my hand on Ring's shoulder. His T-shirt was as completely soaked through as if he had just come out of a swimming pool. As soon as I touched him, he almost jumped out of his skin, almost as if he had forgotten I was there. He was nearing hyperventilation. His right elbow had a bleeding strawberry on it from his tumble, and he was completely disheveled and out of sorts.

"Hey, listen, man, there's a pay phone at that gas station over there. I'll call my dad. Okay?" It was all I could think to say. I had no experience with anything even close to this situation. I didn't wait for his blessing. I simply stood up and then put my hands under his arms and lifted him to his feet. He was wobbling, but he stood without resistance.

I helped him walk to the gas station and I called Dad.

"Son! Where are you?" He was pretty freaked out since I had been gone much longer than I was supposed to be. I explained what had happened the best I could. "I'm on my way," he said.

Ten minutes later, we were both in the car headed back into town.

Ring was no longer sobbing. He had slipped away to some quiet, unresponsive place. He wouldn't speak. He didn't even look up. I rode up front with Dad and Ring rode in the backseat.

We pulled up into the driveway and Mom met us before we could get in the door. She looked at me first, with worry written across her face. Then, after reassuring herself that I was basically intact, she gave all her attention to Ring.

"Come on in, David. Let's get you cleaned up."

He kept his eyes fixed on the ground and walked with tiny, shuffling steps. His dragging feet made a certain sound on the sidewalk that would normally make my skin crawl. At the moment, it was just another odd element in a bizarre evening.

As we came through the front door, Kathy was sitting on the bottom step of the staircase, wearing the worries of the world on her face. She had no idea what was going on, as was true for all of us, and I gave her a little touch of reassurance on the shoulder as we passed her to get to the kitchen.

We sat down at the table and Mom produced a glass of water for Ring. He awkwardly picked it up with both hands and brought it to his mouth, drinking even as droplets poured down his shirt. He made a slurping sound, the likes of which I'd never heard at the table. I hadn't realized it until this moment, but Ring couldn't drink hot beverages like the rest of us. They would burn his lips.

As the liquid hit his lips, he began chugging it between deep, distressed breaths. It was as if a man had just emerged from the desert and found a water hose. I had noticed that Ring never ate in front of people, probably because he had so much trouble eating and talking at the same time. He never said anything about it, but I could tell it embarrassed him. But on this night his guard was down. We were seeing him as he really was.

Mom topped off his glass with more water. “David, maybe you should stay with us tonight.” Her words brought him up short, and he looked up to realize we were all watching him. We weren’t staring on purpose, but I could understand how he would feel suddenly self-conscious. Kathy, who had followed us into the kitchen, now nonchalantly made her way toward the door—with tears in her eyes.

He didn’t answer Mom about staying, so I answered for him. “Mom, Ring could have my room.”

She cut me off. “First of all, he has a first name: David. Second, why don’t you let him decide for himself? He may not want to stay.”

Ring’s face showed a touch of approval; perhaps it was nice for someone to give him credit for having a mind of his own. I thought about the mother he’d lost, and wondered if he was thinking of her now.

“Home.”

That’s all he said. And that settled it; he would not be staying.

I was busy being irritated with Mom for correcting me when I was only trying to help. She now served Ring a still-warm slice of peach pie. I guess she had thrown it in the oven when Dad left the house to come pick us up. It seemed to me an odd action to take in an emergency, but now she was looking like a genius. My irritation faded.

I don’t know if it was the rush of adrenaline or if he just hadn’t eaten in days, but Ring ate that slice in about fifteen seconds, making grunting noises as he did. Crust crumbs were all over his face, accented by a few gobs of shiny stickiness on his chin, cheeks, even his nose. When he finished the first one, Mom brought another. Then another. Then another. I had one too, but Ring devoured the entire pie minus that one piece. It was fascinating, actually.

Dad walked in from the other room and sat down next to Ring. "I just got off the phone with your sister's friend. Debbie, is it? I hoped to speak to Loretta, but Debbie said she was already asleep and not feeling well."

Ring's whole demeanor now changed. The gentle light of comfort had been stealing into it, but now he darkened. There was something crazy in his eyes, and Dad saw it too.

He reached across the table and gently took hold of Ring's forearm. "David, it's okay. I told her you were pretty upset. She said it was okay if you stayed here for a few hours to cool off. Then I can take you home. Everything's okay."

"Bwutha Don, is that aw she said?" It was the first time he had spoken more than one word since trying to deck me out on the highway.

"Yep. That's all she said. Is there something else I need to know?"

Ring wiped his mouth with the back of his hand, and then wiped his hand on his blue jeans—double knit jeans he had found at the thrift store in town. He stared off at something none of us could see. Finally he answered. "No, suh."

I figured Dad and Mom would continue trying to talk to him, to pull out some information—but drawing from some reservoir of parental instinct, they backed off. The two of them simply made sure he'd had enough to eat, then a little while later Dad loaded him up and took him home.

"Night, Ring," I said, standing by the door. He simply nodded back.

I had trouble sleeping that night. Everything just seemed off-balance. I craved resolution, but I couldn't put a puzzle together when most of the pieces were missing.

The total picture may have been hidden from me, but that was all right, because it was about to be changed completely. Radically. Miraculously.

11

September 1961

"What do you mean you can't 'make special concessions' for his condition? Isn't that your job?"

Leron was absolutely furious. As a strong woman and mother, she was not afraid to raise her voice. This was the growl of a momma bear defending her cub.

"Mrs. Ring, we've been over this already. Your son is not in a special education class. For that reason, we cannot spare the staff or resources to help with everything he needs. Mrs. Snidefield is doing all she can to keep up with everyone in her class, which is already past full. David is just going to have to do the best he can in the situation he's in. He'll just have to make his own way."

Well, that was something Leron knew all about. She couldn't remember anything other than making her own way, getting what she could without any kind of help. She hadn't even been told what her child's problem was until she'd lived with eighteen months of it. And even then, it was only by accident that the diagnosis of cerebral palsy had been delivered.

The boy had come down with pneumonia, and he wasn't recovering at a normal pace. Leron had been half frantic. A trip to the doctor brought out the information that those eighteen minutes without oxygen had done permanent damage to the boy's brain. But despite his condition, Leron always pushed him to "make his own way," as they called it now—to live life as normally as he possibly could. She took the phrase "special needs" and dropped the second word, concentrating on teaching her son that he was *special*.

Today, in this unhappy conference, Leron could see that the principal was left to enforce a policy he didn't really like. It was simply an impossible situation. David Ring had originally been placed in a special education school, but he didn't fit there either. They could say what they wanted about the damage to his brain, but the truth was that there was nothing wrong with this boy's cognitive, intellectual, or reasoning faculties. He was a rarity among people with cerebral palsy—his disability was purely physical, a sharp young mind inside a damaged frame.

As a matter of fact, only three weeks into the special school, Leron had gotten a call. That principal had wanted her to know that her son was teaching the teachers. He wasn't just keeping up—he was pulling out in front and leaving the others behind. It seemed more like special gifts than special needs.

So David Ring was placed into regular classes, which worked out pretty well through first and second grade. He could do the work, but pacing was definitely a problem. His fumbling fingers and shuffling feet made his assignments drag on far too long. Even so, he got by until he had to move to a different school for third grade.

His new third-grade teacher allowed him extra time in class to get things finished. The only problem was that this allotted time came during recess. So while all the other children were swinging from monkey bars or booting kick balls into the outfield—letting off the excess steam that every child had—David was at a small school desk working through his assignments with the speed of an inchworm.

For several days, he finished just as the bell rang, signaling the end of recess. The other boys and girls would pour into the classroom laughing, screaming, and rambunctious. Before now, David had not taken in the full implications of what it meant to be different from others. Now he could see. There was a whole world of running, playing, laughing, and fast chatter to which he would never gain entry. Those doors were barred, and he felt a despondency unusual for a child in third grade. He would have to make his own way. His mother had told him so, and he knew it was true.

Leron also felt the chill of isolation. Oscar was really gone, even if she had decided she wanted him back. Life never seemed to sort itself out. And faith? What was the point of it, if it never seemed to pay off? What God would afflict a sweet boy and then give him no breaks in life? Why had he brought him back to life in the delivery room, if this was the only life available to him? How could anyone say God was good?

She never openly rejected God or her faith, but the reality of her doubt took on solidity until it defined her. She wasted no more time on prayers since they never made it past the ceiling anyway. She stopped looking at life as something with meaning, something leading upward. She evened out into reality instead: the bitter truth was that she had to make her own way, and so did everyone else. God's way led to nothing but empty wilderness. Her love would have to be enough for David.

And it was. So thoroughly did she cherish and nourish him with affection that he felt a fullness, the same happiness that any other child would feel. Until those moments in the classroom after recess, he had never felt there was anything good in life he was missing.

Leron fought for him. She believed in him. She provided for him, even to the occasional Baby Ruth—milk chocolate paint on the canvas of his little face. She did not love every minute of her life, but she loved every minute of him—messes, stutters, limps, and all.

"David," she would say, "you don't have to worry about how other kids can walk or run. Being different is your gift, so don't be afraid of it."

He would lie in her arms for hours. Her "cuddle bug," she called him. And the stress of her financial woes and time constraints would for a moment melt away. The two of them provided enough light for each other that the world's darkness could never truly encroach.

One day after school, she took him to the candy store in the middle of the old square in Jonesboro. It was a rainy afternoon, but the storm system had cleared a bit, leaving splashes of blue sky between the thick gray clouds and a heavy humidity that brought beads of sweat even when there was no sunshine.

As they approached the store, they suddenly heard someone shouting on the other side of the street. "You oughta know better, ya little idiot!" They turned just in time to see an old white man, probably sixty or more, holding a little black boy by the collar of his shirt. The little boy couldn't have been more than six or seven—almost David's age. The old man was jerking him around so hard that his shirt looked like it could rip at any minute. He tugged the boy up on his tiptoes and shouted directly into his face.

The little boy was alone, and his eyes were wide with terror. "I'm sorry, Mista—I was just thirsty, that's all. I pwomise that's all."

"Thirsty? You was thirsty, huh? I guess you can't read either, can you?" The man was stumbling, swaying, slurring his speech, and he clutched a small brown paper bag in his other hand. Clearly he'd been sipping from it for some time.

Above the scene was a sign in black and white that read "Whites Only." Just below it was a water fountain.

David stared at the spectacle with amazement and terror. He was completely frozen in his tracks. "Momma? What—" He broke off when he turned and saw that his mother wasn't there.

The man across the street then grabbed the little boy's ears and began to yell more obscenities into his face. The boy screamed in pain. David then noticed people were gathering—dozens of them, more than you'd have thought were even around—and they were intent on witnessing the scene of terror. A mom with her teenage daughter came, both bearing sacks of groceries. A businessman showed up, dressed to the nines with a black briefcase and shoes so shiny you could almost see your reflection in them.

They all just stood there. Watching. Frozen by something, though David had no idea what it was. There was something more to the event than an old man yelling at a little boy—David was sure of that.

Jonesboro was no Selma, but like most Southern towns of the era, it still teemed with racism. At any rate, such matters were usually handled with more discretion than the old drunk was capable of observing. His actions weren't seen as wrong so much as they were seen as washing dirty linen in public. There were alleyways for this kind of thing.

The old man's face was as red as an angry wasp. He raised a fist in the air, then smashed it against the boy's cheekbone. The boy fell to the ground and covered his face in his hands, screaming at the top of his lungs. "Pwease, mista! Pwease! I'm sorry!" The man doubled over, cradling his hand, his own hand stinging from the blow.

"You shut up or I'll shut you up!" He picked up his foot to kick the little boy, but a sudden push sent the man flying and then stumbling for several more steps until he careened into the water fountain. He let out a peculiar cry—"Woof!" The rounded edge of the stainless steel fountain had gone straight into his ribs, knocking the breath from him.

To David's shock, there was his mother in the center of it all. Leron stood towering over the old man, her blue-and-white polka-dotted dress blowing in the afternoon breeze like a superhero's cape. "Why don't you try kicking someone your own size!"

The old drunk continued writhing in pain on the ground before the fountain, holding his ribs and trying to catch his breath.

Leron was a white woman living in the South. She was far from a civil rights activist, but neither was she one to sit by and let a little boy be assaulted by some drunken beast. She knew what it was like to have a son with no fair chance in life. She was certainly not exempt from the cloud of racism she was raised in, but her own unique experiences as a protective mother broke through the fog in this case, revealing an unexpected light. Being a woman of strength and action, she would not stand by and do nothing.

Leron turned away from the man and reached down for the little boy, who let out a little whimper and instinctively pulled away from her like a wounded foal out in the wild. "It's okay, son. It's okay. I'm not going to hurt you." She gently touched his elbow as she said it. "Where's your momma?"

He didn't answer her. He was shivering as if living in his own private winter. But as she spoke gently to him, she proved that a mother's voice transcends the boundaries of race and culture. He seemed to be drawn to it. Comforted by it. He finally took her hand and she helped him up off the ground. She dusted off his shirt and his little bottom.

"I was just thirsty. That's all," he blubbered, wiping huge strings of snot from his nose onto his sleeve.

She smiled at the appealing little guy, but she had to watch their backs now. "I know, baby. We'll get you a drink."

Then she looked around at the man in the black suit, casting daggers of disdain from her eyes in his direction. He looked back at her and then down at the ground, shrouded in shame. The crowd began to slowly drain away, and Leron walked the little boy across the street to rejoin David.

No more than three minutes passed before the boy's mother showed up, visibly upset and relieved at the same time. Her little boy had wandered off from a playground some seven blocks away. She snatched him up in her arms, crying hysterically. Then she examined his face and saw the red marks from the attack.

She turned to Leron, who immediately began telling her what had happened before she could come to any of her own conclusions. They stood there talking for what seemed like a long time, something you didn't see every day on the streets of Jonesboro in those days.

David and the little boy both decided to plop down next to each other on an old wooden bench on the sidewalk. The bench seat was made out of horizontal slats and was covered in dark stain. It looked as if it had been sat on—and also carved into with knives and keys—by a couple hundred thousand people since the last paintbrush had touched it.

The boys didn't seem to care. It was a fine place to sit. Neither pair of feet touched the ground, dangling back and forth in contented symmetry. The little boy who had been attacked sat fiddling with an old Superman action figure. The blues and reds on the Man of Steel's super outfit were still pretty crisp, but the black outlines of his facial features had long since faded from the elements and the many little hands that had played with the figure.

David kept his gaze downward, but he couldn't help but glance over at the Superman every few seconds. His hands were empty, but his mind was flying that little action figure around in the air, rescuing damsels and toppling buildings. After all, he already knew how to play with something without the complete use of his hands. This was pretty much the same.

"You wike Superman?" the boy suddenly asked. David had not noticed that he had seen him looking at it.

"Yes."

"Do you want to play with it?" He held the toy out to David, whose eyes could not hide the glee every kid feels for something new—even when something new is something old. David accepted the toy graciously, carefully.

The boy watched his shaking fingers try to hold the toy. He turned his head to one side. "What's wong with yo' legs and hands?"

David got that one a lot. Kids don't know all the rules of what should or should not be said.

But David did not retreat into himself like he usually did when the question was asked. In his mind, he was flying through space with Superman. "I have cewebwal pawsy."

The boy laughed a little. "You talk funny!" Though he laughed at David, it was innocently rather than cruelly.

"I know." David smiled as Superman flew a figure-eight. "Yuh do too." He turned and looked at the boy. They both smiled. "I'm David. What's yo name?"

"I'm Supuman!" the boy replied with a grin and two tiny biceps posed next to his equally tiny head.

David's eyes grew to saucer size. "Aw you chocowate Supuhman?"

Superman rolled around on the bench like it was the funniest thing he had ever heard. The giggles were so great that they became contagious, working their way through the air across the bench and into David. Soon the boys were both doubled over laughing hysterically, rolling around all over each other like a couple of little piglets in a mud puddle.

That moment when the boys' uproarious laughter hit its delightful fever pitch, the mothers stopped talking and looked at the children, lost in their own world of play, giggling and hitting and playing heroes and villains with the single toy. These children were not in Jonesboro, nor anywhere in the Deep South. They were somewhere in Metropolis—and they didn't care if they ever came back. For a moment, the whole street seemed to come to a complete standstill. Perhaps even all the busyness in Arkansas had stopped to witness their play.

Then Superman's mother did something Leron did not expect—she hugged Leron. At first, Leron wasn't sure how to hug back, but then it came naturally. After a few good-byes, they all left to get home before it got too dark. Leron took David's hand. "Come on, baby. Let's go get you that candy."

"Momma? Why he huwt him?" Now that they were alone, David's face showed that he was allowing himself to process what had happened on the street earlier.

Leron kept walking as she answered him. "Because he is different, baby. That's all. Sometimes people try to hurt anyone who is different. But different is good. There is nothing wrong with it and that old man was wrong. Wrong, wrong, wrong, baby."

David looked off and squinted at the bright orange and red blazes of the distant sunset. As if the colors themselves were illuminating new compartments in his brain, he took a deep breath and then let it out.

"Momma? I difwent."

"I know, baby."

Her eyes welled up with tears as she said it, but she kept walking, hoping he wouldn't see them. He had made the connection, as much as she wished he had not. It was inevitable. She knew there would be times when he would be on the receiving end of such treatment. And she knew there would also be times she would not be there to rescue him.

Finally, walking wouldn't suffice, so she stopped and pulled him close to try to hide her tears. She said it again.

"I know, baby."

Those were all the words she had. She would fight for him, and fight for him again. But there were limits even to the reach of a mother's insistent love. She wasn't Superman.

12

April 1970

I sat on the bed, rubbed my sleepy eyes, and tried to focus on a new day. It took me a moment to recall the strange occurrences of the night before. I wondered if I would ever hear any kind of explanation, or whether it would all become another small-town hush-hush subject, never to be raised again.

Ambling into the kitchen where Dad was eating his cereal, I sat down next to him and poured a bowl for myself. Strangely, our conversation ignored the obvious current events—just pleasantries and today's agenda. This was an anomaly for life in the Wideman household. We usually talked about everything! I was disappointed. I wanted my dad—my hero—to help fix whatever was wrong. But would it be wrong for me to raise the subject?

I guess he sensed my puzzlement. Just as he stood up to leave for the office, he said, "Son, what is it? What's eating at you?"

"Dad, are you not going to—you know, talk to Ring and figure out what's wrong?" Dad wasn't just Dad; he was Brother Don. He was sort of everybody's dad.

"Not now. Not yet."

Dad seemed to know something I didn't. Yet always the mind reader, he continued, "David, I know exactly as much as you do. But sometimes actions are more important than answers. We can't make answers appear, but we can certainly make actions appear anytime we want."

With that, he quickly gave me a hug and walked to the front door. "Honey, I got a quick appointment at the church," he called to my mother, "and then I'm going to the airport to pick up Bill and Wilma."

It was Wednesday—church night—but I had forgotten such things in the rush of events. Dad was gone already, so I walked into the kitchen where Mom was cooking. "Why is Dad picking up Uncle Bill from the airport?"

"David, don't you remember? The revival with your Uncle Bill starts tonight and goes through Sunday."

"Oh, man!" I groaned. "That means we won't have youth group tomorrow night." It was a typical pastor's kid scenario. The thing we loved most about church was often suspended so we could all come together for the thing we loved least about church—being with the old people.

Mom gave me the look. "David, try to have a good attitude, son! It's just until Sunday and we need to support your father and the whole church, not just the youth group. You get to see all your friends all you want at school."

"Yes, ma'am." There would be no winning on matters such as these. Conceding defeat was the only move.

Mom finished wiping off the counter and met my eye. "And David, I also invited Ring to come to the revival tonight."

"Really?"

I didn't mean it the way it sounded. It just seemed like an empty gesture. Adult revivals were not exactly hot destinations for teenagers, though I loved my uncle Bill. And Ring, well, he was in a unique category of people. If kids like us couldn't get through to him, how was a sermon going to do it?

"Yes. Really." She didn't seem very annoyed with my response, and in the next moment she suddenly became very intent. "David, you just never know what God might do in someone's life. Opportunities are all around us, so we have to take as many as we can."

What could I say to that?

"Yes, ma'am."

I headed off to school as usual. Naturally I kept a close watch for Ring, but I didn't see him in the halls between classes. The cafeteria was my best shot at a sighting, but when lunchtime rolled around, Ring was nowhere to be seen. I asked around, and no one had seen him all day.

I put Ring out of my mind, ready to think of other subjects for a change. After school, I headed to track practice and worked up another good sweat, then took another shower. Then it was home for dinner and getting spiffed up for church. I had strong doubts Mom's specially invited guest would be there, and I wasn't the least surprised to get there and find out I was right. Lots of smiling, chatting members, but no Ring.

No other kids my age, either. I was stuck there by myself. But I was used to that, and besides, the preacher was Uncle Bill, and he was okay by me.

After church, we all went back to our house to eat and catch up. Mom asked me if I knew anything about Ring's whereabouts. I just shrugged my shoulders. I was frankly ready to move on.

Yet the next morning, when he was absent from school again, I couldn't help but notice. And curiosity began to creep back in and take hold of me again. What was up with this guy? Whatever it was, it wasn't my job. Life would go on, and good luck to him. I coasted through the day, and by a quarter to six, I was at church for the second night of the revival. The service didn't actually start until 6:30, but we were on PFST: Pastor's Family Standard Time. We took whatever the start time was for "normal" folks and backed it up at least forty-five minutes.

And we never came early just to sit there and wait for people to arrive. There was always work to be done. Last-second details to attend to. A small pile of debris to sweep up here. A lightbulb to replace there. Communion to prepare—shiny, stainless steel plates and round stackable containers with dozens of holes in them to hold the tiny plastic communion cups, which each needed to be filled with grape juice. In the winter, our tasks also included scraping ice and shoveling snow from the front sidewalk of the church.

I finished up a few last-second tasks, talked with Uncle Bill for a few minutes, and then sat on the second pew on the left side of the center aisle. Standard Wideman location.

The carpet in our sanctuary was classic burnt orange. I considered it quite hideous most of the time, but on afternoons like this one, the sun would shine through the windows on the west side of the building and the orange seemed to come alive in some weird way. It required direct afternoon sunlight to be tolerated.

The service began, as usual, with the singing of hymns. But when we hit the third verse of "I Will Sing the Wondrous

Story," I detected a new, unexpected object in my periphery. I turned my head to see Ring awkwardly inching his way past the people at the end of my pew. I couldn't believe it, and honestly I didn't really want it. I was in no mood to be around this guy. I had basically saved his life and he'd been missing for two days.

He glanced at me momentarily as he turned to face forward. His demeanor had not really changed since I had last seen him. In fact, it was somehow worse. I didn't want to acknowledge him, but Dad's voice had some kind of hiding place inside me, and it would come out at times like this and whisper what I knew was the right thing to do. I sighed inwardly, leaned over, and whispered, "You okay?"

My reward for "the right thing," of course, was his dark-cloud reply: "Whadda yuh think?" It just never got any better with this guy.

I chased Dad's inner voice back into its corner and hissed, "You don't have to be such a jerk. A simple 'thanks for saving my life' would do."

He had been looking forward the whole time, but now he turned toward me. The intense afternoon light flooding in from the window made him squint, and he held his hand up to shade his face and said, "Yuh shoulduh jus' wemme die!"

He didn't have the close control of his voice that most of us have, and he'd spoken a little louder than he had intended. We both realized that several elderly pairs of eyes were now staring at us.

We faced back forward, but I wasn't done. I needed the last word. "You can't keep living like this."

"I don' wanna live."

Just then, my father stepped to the pulpit and closed the song service in prayer, preparing to introduce Uncle

Bill. We sat down, but we didn't acknowledge each other's existence.

I imagined that if I could string together every minute I had ever sat through a church service, I had spent upwards of six months of my childhood sitting through song services and sermons. And it was not that they didn't interest me at all; they actually did. I was one of those pastor's kids who had connected with the message my dad offered every week. I was sincerely trying to live what I understood to be the Christian life. I was no rebel against the cause.

Still, all the demands of being in a ministerial family could be hard to bear. It meant sitting through every single service and being the first there and the last to leave. For an active teenager, it could be a little too much of the same thing. I had put in six accumulated months of pew-dwelling, but I could rarely tell you what had happened or what was said on any particular occasion—unless it was something truly spectacular like Sister Nancy "crop dusting" the congregation or Brother Harold, the victim of a faulty hearing aid, unknowingly shouting at his wife that he'd heard this message a hundred times before. The more ordinary stuff? I believed it and I tried to live it, but I didn't necessarily stay dialed in every week to every minute detail.

This was one of those occasions when I didn't have the emotional energy to follow every word of the sermon or turn to every Scripture reference. I loved Uncle Bill, but this had been some kind of week. What I really needed was to blow off some steam, but you can't do that in the second pew on the left-hand aisle. So instead I blew off steam mentally. My mind wandered freely over every area of my life, every interest. Friends, school, sports, girls. I wandered so far that I took a left turn into dreamland and dozed off, violating one of the most serious Wideman family commandments.

Who knows how long I was out? It was the out-of-tune Baldwin piano that brought me back from my little hike into the Land of Nod.

I wonder how many saints over the years have awakened to a congregational singing of "Just As I Am"? Just as I am, without one plea. No plea, no excuse for falling asleep right in front of my Uncle Billy. I thrashed through the pages of the hymnal to the right place, and lifted my groggy voice. Furtively peeking to see if I'd been caught, I saw—or didn't see—something startling. No Ring beside me.

Well, he'd probably taken his dark cloud and gone on home. That would be just about typical for him. I looked back at the hymnal, tried to look awake and alert—and heard someone crying at the altar. *What?*

I looked up and there was Ring, kneeling and praying in the comforting embrace of my dad and my uncle. He was rocking back and forth, and tears were flooding down his cheeks.

Dad met my eye and beckoned. He wanted me to join them.

13

May 1968

Leron had not wanted to admit it, maybe because the possibility of what could be wrong was just too much to face. Besides, she had dwelt on worst-case scenarios before and all that did was waste a whole lot of emotional energy over what turned out to be nothing.

But it had been months now. She knew somewhere deep inside that this was not "nothing."

Four years earlier, pain in her left breast had come upon her suddenly. The doctor found a tumor and removed it. There was every assurance they'd gotten everything. So she had moved on and lived her life. No chemotherapy. No other treatments. Just life as usual.

But this was different. There was a knot in her neck, and it had come up quickly. It was clearly not nothing. On the other hand, Leron was Southern Mom tough. She kept the world spinning for her David, with his countless doctor visits. Endless hours. Sleepless nights. She could beat this, whatever it was. She could beat it. She had to beat it—too much was riding on her shoulders.

Unfortunately, such self-affirmations didn't do the trick this time. She finally went to her family physician, who had treated her children countless times, and very soon could tell he was trying to conceal his real level of concern. His face gave it away, despite all his practiced, reassuring comments.

"Let's not worry before we need to. Let's wait and see what the tests reveal," he said.

During the process of waiting there was a new kind of pain, and the doctors couldn't find its source. From the pit of her stomach came a churning and nagging ache, and it continued through the tests, scans, pricks, pokes, and prods. They took out a few lymph nodes to test them. She had to go to Little Rock for the procedure. St. Bernard's was too small to handle the specialized needs of this case.

The few days afterward were agonizing. She had to be home, caring for her children, especially her special angel who was growing so big. It was easy to keep busy—it would be impossible not to—but her nerves were on edge all the time, waiting for the phone to ring. For years, she had expected the terrible news about her first husband. Now the phone threatened to bring bad tidings for her as well.

So now more than ever, she delighted in Judy and David, the children who were still at home with her. Their laughter, their silliness, even their feistiness. They were teenagers, old enough to instinctively detect the severity of the situation. Still, she was their momma. She soothed their fears, reassured them that she was always there for them. But her stomach hurt. All the while, it hurt.

Finally the phone rang. Leron picked it up. She murmured a few "yeses" and "I sees," then put the receiver back in its place.

Cancer.

Who could say where it came from? Maybe they hadn't gotten it all a few years ago, and it had spread to her lymph nodes. The one certain fact was that she had no chance. The clock was now ticking for Leron, this once-indestructible, all-protecting mother of her children.

During the next few months, she was in and out of the hospital. David stayed with one of his older brothers, then one of his sisters, wherever there was a relative willing to give him a meal and a place to lay his head. He didn't know why he was being swapped between homes. He didn't know why he suddenly couldn't see his mother. But he picked up on the hushed voices in other rooms, his mother's name whispered with sadness. Something was terribly wrong; the center of his universe was a great, gaping hole. And for the first time, his emotions became as difficult to control as his hands or his mouth.

Leron missed him just as painfully, and she was filled with regrets and unanswered questions. What if she had done things differently—gone to the doctor sooner? Would it have made any difference? And who would pay the hospital bills?

But two questions swallowed up all the others: Where was God? And who would care for David?

David wasn't a little boy anymore; he was almost fifteen. He had not quite reached his full height, but things were different. When he was smaller, people seemed to have more tolerance for his condition, out of pity. In general, people pity small, cute things more than full-grown things.

But Leron knew that as David's body grew, so would the world's cruelty. Teenagers would no doubt eat him for lunch.

Adults too. He didn't know this yet. His mind was quite sharp, thus in theory he should have ascertained the altitude of the insurmountable peak he was trying to climb with one proverbial hand tied behind his back, but he didn't. He didn't know, because the only reality he lived in was the safe version his mother had created for him. It was like her love—her hope for him eclipsed everything else he experienced, even when it was harsh or cruel. Still, know it or not, he was headed up that mountain.

Leron was the one carrying him. She was his world. His provision. His encouragement. His forgiver. His advocate. His liaison to other people. She was everything, so up to this point in life he had been able to smile and put his head down, focusing on today's tiny step instead of the impasse looming before him. She knew that the day was now fast approaching when he would have to raise his own head—and he was going to see something she could not bring herself to face.

J. D. was surprised when she asked him to stay home and watch the kids while she went out. They were old enough to watch themselves, but it made her feel better to have an adult around. David was not used to being alone, and he still required so much care for even the tiniest tasks. Then again, he was unlikely to let J. D. help.

It wasn't as if Leron wanted to go out on the town and sow some final wild oats. She was going out to search for the answer to that first vital question.

Where was God?

When she'd first turned away from her faith, she felt a certain bold confidence that her actions were justified. The cloud of pain had grown too intense to see God through, and she figured he had run out of interest in her.

The most logical mind would assume that the doctor's report would only reinforce those feelings. Yet against all odds—amid the greatest agony of body and mind imaginable—she instead felt something drawing her. Even calling to her. It didn't make any sense, but it was undeniable.

Surprisingly, the feeling was not coming from a place of guilt. She felt uncertainty, sure, but there was an almost tangible peacefulness to it. Like a whisper from an old friend. At first she tried to ignore these tentative feelings of faith because they seemed so out of place in her situation. But no matter how loud it was inside the house or inside her head, the whisper persisted. It wouldn't go away.

God? Are you there? The question chipped away at her. Soon she found herself losing the boldness with which she had denounced her faith. She thought of J. D. and the mistake she had justified all these years, and for the first time she stopped thinking of the impossible situation she'd been in. She could be truly honest with herself. It didn't seem worth taking the effort to defend her actions anymore.

She even thought of Oscar, a man whom she had allowed to shoulder the blame for so much. No matter what she had done, he'd loved her and the kids, and she knew she had pushed him away. His road had not been easy either. He had by no means been completely in the right, but he'd been willing to try. She had missed that fact those years before. She began to see that she was running out of time to hold on to certain kinds of things.

She knew there would always be people to blame—and that her children, especially David, would face their own villains. She would no longer be the shade tree to block out the blistering sun and keep them from being scorched. And that whisper kept coming. *Is that you, God?*

She set out that night to find the whisper and to see if it was real. Or was her mind simply playing a cruel game of hide and seek with her? Perhaps the guilt and stress had grown too great and a neuron was pressing against a synapse or something.

Or perhaps it was real. She would never know until she looked.

She really didn't know of any other place to go except to a little church she knew very well. Painfully so. She returned not just to her roots but to the very place that a root of resentment in her marriage had first begun to burrow into the soil of her soul. Woods Chapel—the church Oscar had once pastored. That was the scene of the crime for her, the place her faith had undergone its first attack.

She was late to the service, so she climbed the concrete steps and slipped into the back, trying to remain undetected.

But the whisper would have none of it! The moment she crossed that threshold, it was as if the whisper became a loud voice within her. The pastor was a young man she had never seen before, but his identity was inconsequential to her. He was about halfway through his sermon, which sounded like incoherent noises in her ears. The church was filled with pink and yellow hats on the heads of women wearing pink and yellow dresses, and each one seemed to be a part of an elaborate plan to wave their fans in unison. It was a hot night for May.

The message was the last thing she was experiencing, or at least she thought, until suddenly the pastor's words stopped sounding like someone gargling in the other room. The meaning of his words began to break through, resonating in her ears as if she were sitting in the front row at Carnegie Hall.

"Just like with Joseph, there is not a hole deep enough—even if you helped to dig it—where God's whisper of grace cannot be heard!"

This was the message, though she heard a lot more words and ideas. This was all that mattered. She couldn't recall taking even one step, but she looked up to find herself at the altar, surrounded by people she didn't know at all. The pastor knelt beside her and put his hand on her shoulder.

The tears were almost blinding, yet as she peeked through them at the crowd of people, all praying out loud and singing over her, she had the strangest thought. All those arms resembled the branches of a tree. She looked at the floor, and even there she could see the shadows of the arms raised over her. It was so very peaceful.

Then the pastor prayed softly over her: "He shall hide you in the shadow of his wings."

She rested in the shadow of that tree as the branches whispered above her in the breeze. It was cooling to the scorched blisters of her soul. The winds of redemption just kept coming, and she felt clean. Whole. At peace.

She had no idea how long she was there, but the shadow she found there was one she knew would continue to shade her, no matter what she was going to have to face. It was not the dark cloud she had felt hovering over her since her heart began pulling away so many years before. Rather, it was like the cloud that guided God's people in the desert.

Yes, they were in the desert—as was she. And she now knew that God had been there with her the entire journey. He cared for her blisters.

And more importantly, she felt a peace that the same shadow she was now living under—and, yes, dying under—would also cover her David. She would not have to be his only shade tree. There would be another available to him, if he would only follow the same whisper. Like so many other things, it was beyond her control. But not beyond hope.

A group of strangers stretched out their branches over her that night, sheltering her with their hands and prayers. It was something she thought she would never see, yet it changed the course of her days.

14

April 17, 1970

In our little church, a group of strangers were gathered around Ring that night, sheltering him with their hands and prayers. It was something I thought I would never see, yet it changed the course of his days.

It also changed the course of mine.

I walked toward them, as my dad had motioned for me to do, yet I felt as if I were still asleep and dreaming. It was hard to believe that only a couple of nights before I had followed Ring out to the interstate off-ramp. He had been so resistant for so long, and honestly, I wasn't sure that this was an indicator of any changes.

I was only about fifteen feet away from the group of people praying around Ring, but it took me quite some time to get to him. I had to maneuver through the crowd like a salmon swimming upstream. Everyone's eyes were closed, and they were praying so intently that I really hated to disturb them. But I had to get to the middle. I needed to be a part of this moment.

I was struck by the genuineness of the people from our church. Most of those who showed up on a weeknight revival were older folks. Lots of white hair, a few canes here and there. We often had a lot of kids from the football and basketball teams and from school show up at our youth group on Thursday nights; only a fraction of them would ever get up early on a Sunday to come to a church like ours. Or anyone's, I suppose.

I did not dislike the older people in our church, but neither did I call up Brother Melvin on a weekly basis to go grab a soda down at Begg's. I didn't wish any of them any harm, yet now I realized I was part of a generation gap.

I think I had even let resentment toward them find safe harbor in some parts of my mind. Again, it was not malicious. If anything it was barely conscious. I didn't notice it until I had to gently push my way through that crowd of older people praying for my friend Ring. They had always seemed so obstinate. So distant. Not only uninterested in us younger people but also annoyed by our very presence.

Our hair was always too long. Our music was always too loud. Our clothes were always too casual. As a preacher's kid, I was strictly taught to be kind to everyone, to say, "Yessir" and "No, ma'am." To hold the door open and smile. To keep my room clean because we never knew when a patron of the parsonage might show up for an uninvited "visit"—that is, to inspect said parsonage.

Even though we had a very good church situation, I had still witnessed my parents dealing with the stress of this job. These people. The one person who decided to critique the theological soundness of Dad's message. The phone call reminding my mother that she had forgotten to send food to someone sick. My sister and I had seen the pressure, even though our parents tried hard to hide it from us.

My parents didn't want their kids to resent their calling to serve people. Dad used to say that if you want to be used by God, then you'll be used by people. But in the real world of teenage life, I never warmed to the idea that the people I loved most in life would be used by the people I loved less.

I realized all these thoughts and resentments as I made my way toward Ring. I could hear the whispers of these people. Their words of love spoken for a boy they didn't know from Adam. As I kept pressing through the crowd, I saw tears running down wrinkled cheeks. And I began to see past the chasm—to see that perhaps, even though they had legitimately offended or even blatantly wronged my family at times, they were another kind of family to me. They were worth loving.

It was obvious too that they loved Ring. The resentment began falling off of me like flakes of snow from a tree struck by a winter breeze. And by the time I reached Ring, the resentment was gone, though it came back for regular visits.

It was as if that short journey from the pew through these people had cleansed me of things I didn't know were making me dirty.

When I reached Ring, he was not kneeling. He was lying on his stomach with his hands covering his face, which was buried in the orange carpet. This had never happened in our church before. We were Baptists and kneeling was the go-to posture for prayer. But this was not just a prayer—this was life and death. And somehow, it seemed that the people who surrounded us sensed this as well.

He was not just crying. He was wailing, completely undone. Each guttural cry seemed to come in waves, as if they were layered deep in his soul, cries of anguish going back to the day he was born. And the people around him were pulling out wave after wave, until all was spent.

Ring raised himself up at last and sat, his knees raised in front of him. Sister Ethel handed him a handkerchief to wipe his nose. He blew it instead and then handed the soiled fabric back to her—which she calmly took and tucked into her little purse. Even in this sacred moment, I couldn't help but feel that this was gross—and my newfound respect for these people just increased again.

Ring rested his arms on his knees and just sat there for a few minutes more, eyes still closed. Then he wiped his eyes with the back of his hands and turned to look at me. It was a different Ring. Obviously, he was technically the same Ring—but he was different. And I don't mean like when a person takes a vacation and someone says, "You look like a different person! You really must have needed a break."

I mean it looked as if he'd taken a vacation to heaven. His face may have been a mess, but his eyes showed me a whole new person. The angry fight had gone out of his eyes.

When it was obvious he was finished praying and ready to stand, Dad and I helped him to his feet. Then the whole circle of people, who had stayed with him through tears and anguish for over an hour, broke out into applause. There couldn't have been more than fifteen or twenty people, but it sounded like a whole stadium was applauding. They had surrounded Ring in his moment of need and now they were surrounding him with their support for the future.

A few hours later I was sitting with Uncle Bill, Dad, and Ring at our house. Mom had gone out to Begg's and had brought back an assortment of sodas for everyone. A special treat. I had cherry. Ring went with root beer. Mom brought him a straw this time, since we knew how hard it was for him to drink without one. She also picked up a box of crackers and a block of cheese for snacking. This particular combo was a staple at the Wideman house after an evening church service.

It was one of the most surreal moments in my life. I knew it was the beginning of something different not just for Ring but for our family too. During that gathering he became a part of us forever.

I had always listened in Sunday school and even read the Bible for myself. The best way to describe Ring was as Luke described the violent and naked crazy man who lived in the graveyard and terrorized people, the one from whom Jesus cast out over a thousand demons: "He was clothed and in his right mind."

I do not mean that Ring ever had demons inside to cast out; I simply mean the difference between Ring before that night and after it was striking and drastic. He still walked the same. He still talked the same. But his words and his steps were somehow not the same.

Dad did most of the talking that night. Ring really didn't have much to say. We all knew that the loss of his mother had really hit him hard, but it still seemed like something else had been tormenting him. He didn't say what it was. Yet whatever it was, Ring now seemed to possess an outlook I had never imagined I would ever see on his face: hope.

Dad was masterful with his words, speaking to Ring as he would have spoken to me. Ring looked him in the eyes, something I was not used to seeing him do. Three root beers later, he was still listening. I guess he was pretty thirsty and

Dad was pretty talkative. Either way, I didn't care if we ever left that little square table.

Dad talked to him about what it meant to follow after Jesus. He told him that God would always hear his prayers, and that no matter what happened from that point forward, he should always run to Jesus in good times and bad.

These were all things I had heard my dad preach or tell to other people a hundred times before, but that night they seemed to be even more alive and powerful than usual. They made sense to me—and I even found myself re-embracing them for myself in a way I never knew I could.

When our sodas were gone, Dad looked at Ring and said, "Son, one more thing. I don't know what's going on at home or what all you are facing, but I know it's pretty big stuff."

Ring never broke eye contact with Dad. His face seemed to intensify with each word Dad spoke, but he did not lose his peaceful expression.

Dad continued. "Listen, what happened tonight does not mean you won't face more horrible things in your future. Even tomorrow. You shouldn't expect life to be a cakewalk all of a sudden."

"Yes, suh," Ring said respectfully.

Dad smiled, and then tears filled his eyes. "But from here on out, you do not have to face whatever you have faced alone. We will be there for you—like family. You never have to run away. You never have to give up hope. God loves you—and we love you too. Our house is now your house. Our table is your table. And it's not going anywhere. Okay?"

One last tear—this time of joy—broke free from the corner of Ring's eye.

"Yes, suh. I unduhstand."

15

April 18, 1970—The Next Day

The bell rang and once again the hallway was flooded with people.

Summer break was in sight and our junior year was almost over. The hallways of Liberty High School always smelled different during the last few weeks of school. It was the smell of freedom.

Or maybe it was another smell. At the beginning of the school year, students came to school ready to make a good first impression—meaning they actually took showers. By the end of the year, when time droned on and teachers grated upon the patience of the student body, I think that this student body became less and less cognizant of personal hygiene.

For me, junior year was by far the most enjoyable year of high school. Juniors had the best of all worlds. They had enough freedom and responsibility to stay out later, drive cars, and even go on dates, if there were willing participants. Juniors were rarely picked on; the seniors generally went after the freshmen.

By junior year, the awkward transition between adolescence and adulthood was usually at least in decline. And occasionally, when it came to looks, it had been delightfully vanquished. Those who exited those big, metal doors at the end of the main hallway as mere sophomore girls would now re-cross the same threshold as junior women. And the differences between girls and women were the stuff of high school locker room legend.

Then there was the shaving factor. Junior guys could use a razor with legitimate cause. Whiskers meant real manhood, or so we told ourselves.

There was always the occasional late bloomer who was still waiting on that elusive male growth spurt to grant him a few more inches of height, a few more muscles to fill out his T-shirt, and a few more key changes in his voice so he might sound less like Mary Poppins when he asked a girl on a date. The worst was when one's larynx would mutiny against the rest of the body and suddenly crack in the middle of a sentence. It was hard to maintain any credibility when your voice couldn't even stay steady enough to finish a sentence. Cruel pubescent transition.

Just reach junior year and you knew most of these crises were behind you. Me, I was pretty much in the clear. I was tall enough and filled out enough. When I put on my basketball uniform and glanced at the mirror, I thought I looked more like a man playing the game than a little boy in a peewee league. In comparison, sometimes an underdeveloped freshman or sophomore looked like a marshmallow wearing a tank top and shorts, running around on two toothpicks for legs and carrying a death wish to get clobbered by full grown men on the open court. The growth spurt was the greatest advantage for our survival.

Juniors could dream of college and the future, but at a safe distance. Seniors, on the other hand, started out the year seemingly excited, but that excitement was usually squelched pretty quickly as the realization and pressure of all the big decisions began coming to a head. College admissions and scholarship deadlines loomed over them like prison sentences. Every five minutes, someone was asking, "What do you want to do with the rest of your life?"

And so someone not even twenty years old was expected to decide what they wanted to do every day for a lifetime four times as long as what they had lived up to that point. The pressure generally made them want to explode.

Juniors? Not so. We were on top of the world—and still had a full year to remain there before reality would try to bring us "back down to earth."

That year taught me that I loved US history and that I hated chemistry. The scenery was better in history.

I was not a girl-crazy kind of guy. I dated here and there, but I had no interest in getting serious. There was still way too much life to live for that. But I was still a guy—and our breed relished the moment when a new girl would move into town during the school year. Angelique caught my eye the moment she sat down in the desk next to me in the back of the room in US history during second period. Though I preferred brunettes, her blonde beauty was well worth beholding and admiring.

By this point in our high school careers, my buddies and I had long since faced and conquered our fears of talking to girls. Well, I guess there were little bits of fear still lurking, but we had determined through experience that it was better to face it like a man and get it over with than freeze up and miss an opportunity. And besides, the more times you would courageously charge into that dark abyss wherein the possibilities of embarrassment and rejection were piled high and deep, the more your confidence would build and the less you would look like a fool on the next charge.

And now, with the fair Angelique in my peripheral vision, it was once more into the breach for me. I fumbled with my pencil, rotating its six smooth sides between my fingers. I had yet to sharpen it, but at this point, Ms. Gipson was still shuffling mounds of papers and trying to pass out textbooks.

I didn't waste much time, as that could cause a guy to freeze up—like standing too long at the top of the high dive. It's just going to seem higher and higher the longer you stand there until soon you think you're jumping off the St. Louis Arch. I cleared my throat and turned toward her.

"Hey, you new around here?"

She seemed pretty nervous, yet grateful someone had broken the ice. She smiled, but it was a courtesy smile—showing no teeth—meaning she was still uncomfortable. "Yeah, does it show?"

I smiled back at her on the same level—lip smiling. I held up my pencil. "It could be worse. You could be trying to write with a pencil that literally has no point. It took me two blank pages of notes to figure out I'm an idiot."

All of her gorgeous pearly whites now revealed themselves as she laughed out loud. She suddenly realized her volume and covered her mouth, but kept giggling quietly. It was one of those beautiful moments when a person reveals who they are, even while trying to hide.

"You're hilarious. I'm Angelique."

"I'm David. David Wideman."

That was the extent of our conversation, because Ms. Gipson had begun passing out study guides for the test. The rest of the class was spent taking notes on Andrew Jackson's reasons for shutting down the Bank of the United States—a topic even history teachers obviously thought was boring.

Every once in a while, I would glance over at Angelique. Most of the time, she kept her eyes forward on the teacher. But once she looked back at me and smiled just a bit. The game was afoot. She was "the girl next door" kind of pretty, the kind I liked. If a girl was much prettier than that, she was probably going to be too pretty for the likes of me.

A young man had to be realistic.

The day progressed and lunch finally came. It was also one of the only breaks from the rigmarole of all things academic. It was almost as if the educational system really thought the point of being at school was to learn. We knew better.

Besides gym class, lunch was one of those moments when books were closed and mouths were open—for eating and talking. And much like at my church, the seating arrangement mattered. In my church, where people sat in "their" pews held an importance second only to salvation itself and perhaps the sacraments.

The same held true for the school cafeteria. The first day meant seeing who shared the lunch hour with you, and carefully approaching them nonchalantly—so as to not spook them or appear overeager—and then secure a spot that would remain your spot for the rest of the school year.

This was serious business we were dealing with. In fact, if this experience were to go poorly for one reason or another, you could end up being a wandering lunch nomad, spending lunch periods immemorial betwixt the tables, like a beggar or a leper in some nation made up of adolescents and their meat loaf.

But by this time in the year, lunch was a cinch. Jeff and Tim were both in my lunch period. We went through the line together. The second lunch lady was always the most important in this process because she usually doled out whatever starchy side dish would accompany our protein for the day. Today was Salisbury steak—a school classic. Meat drenched in gravy. Brain food, or something of the sort. The portion dispensed was beyond one's control. Everyone was going to get exactly the same amount—one piece. Done.

But the second lunch lady was the one with the power. She held the mashed potato scoop—a singular utensil of no precision. It could serve any kind of portion. No one knew if it was random or planned, but my buddies and I had concluded that the quantity of potatoes she would put on our trays was directly proportionate to her personal opinion of us. Thus when we reached her part of the line, we were transformed from high school boys to delightful hosts.

"Good afternoon, Mrs. Hopstetler! You look lovely today."

Her smirk and eye-roll became as standard a feature of her uniform as her hairnet. "Thank you, Mr. Wideman."

That smirk seemed to overflow onto her scoop and we walked out of the lunch line with heaping portions of mashed potatoes—which made for fine sleeping during fifth period.

We sat down together at our usual table in the corner of the room and began chowing down and sharing the events of the day. Then, across the room, I saw Ring walk out of the cafeteria line. He was moving slower, obviously, than everyone else. It looked as if he would spill his lunch tray at any moment as he jostled it about, but against all odds he somehow navigated the sea of students without going overboard. Awkward, but successful.

So far that school year, he had been sitting with Bill Shiffle and his crew. I had not spoken to the guys about what had happened at church the night before. I wasn't hiding it, but I guess I wanted to let Ring be the one to tell people whatever he wanted to tell them.

I looked across the room and saw Shiffle. Ring was not walking toward his table. He was walking toward ours—sort of. It kind of seemed like he was back in the middle of the "first day of school cafeteria staking and claiming process" all over again—and now he was squinting about for the hardest part of the whole shenanigan: finding someone to sit with. Someone who would actually want to sit with him.

"Well, here we go," Tim said, rolling his eyes.

Out of the three of us, Tim had had the hardest time connecting with Ring. He was not a bad guy at all. Honestly, Ring was the one who had burned the bridges between the two of them. We all knew that I had a special interest in reaching out to Ring. Jeff had grown weary of the whole thing, just as I had, but since he was pretty much at my side the entire time, he kind of rose and fell with whatever I did. Besides, we both had my dad giving us "pep talks" about compassion and tea bags and such.

Tim was just more likely to tell it like it was. No sugarcoating. The hard thing was that up to that point, Ring had been the same way, probably worse. Sugarcoat? He would dip the whole thing in Tabasco sauce. The result was quite the butting of heads between the two—and a whole lot of indigestion.

Tim was over Ring's sour disposition much quicker than Jeff and me. So anytime we would drag Ring along to a game or a youth group function or anything of the sort, Tim would usually throw out some smart-aleck quip then retire to the other side of the room or field to engage in conversation with more agreeable folk. I was certain that Ring noticed it, but he returned the insult with an even greater insult: apathy.

No one likes to be treated with rudeness or contempt, but in the teenage world (and most other worlds as well) there is no greater slap in the face than to ignore someone—to act as if they mean so little to you that even their negative actions don't register on your radar.

Such a figurative slap was worse than the literal kind. Ring had dealt this out to Tim, and instead of turning the other cheek, Tim was ignoring him right back. And I figured if the two of them had gotten down to some real slapping, we'd all have felt better about it.

So it was no surprise that Tim did not want a rude Ring meandering his way to our table. He had given up on Ring changing.

"Come on, man. We can't let him sit alone," Jeff said.

"I don't see why not," Tim replied. "He's made his bed, now he can lie in it."

I moved over a seat, making room between Jeff and I. In my mind, Tim was not getting to make this decision for all of us. "Dude, it's just lunch. You don't have to take him to prom or anything."

Tim didn't argue with me. I guess I gave the impression that it wouldn't help to do so anyway.

"Ring!" I raised my voice to get his attention. "Over here!" The look on his face was one of absolute relief. He didn't have to act like he wasn't walking toward us now. He plopped down his tan tray quite loudly on the smooth-topped cafeteria table and then took the seat between Jeff and me. "Hey, yuh guys. How's it goweeng?"

Tim looked up at him with a surprised yet still stern expression. He had never heard Ring say anything that remotely resembled something friendly. He was seeing the new Ring for the first time, but I could tell he was not just skeptical but also resistant. I tried to brave the rapids before they had a chance to get out of control.

"Man, it's going great. You should see this new girl in my history class, Angelique." I described her to the guys with vivid, teenage boy detail. Everyone hung on my every word. Everyone, that is, except Tim.

Tim loaded his fork with mashed potatoes and looked directly at Ring as he answered me. "Be careful, David," Tim interrupted, "people aren't always what they seem. Sometimes you can be nice to them and find out they are nothing but total jerks and not worth your time at all."

Jeff was the one rolling his eyes now. "Tim, really, man? I just want to eat my slop in peace."

Oddly enough, Ring did not seem upset at all by Tim's words. In fact, his face did not even resemble the face I had first seen at the bus stop the previous autumn. His face was somewhat lifted now. I don't mean like a facelift someone goes to a surgeon for when they get a double chin or wrinkles. I mean his expression was just raised. When I asked Dad about it later, he said that it was a "change in his countenance." He had noticed it too. Same blue eyes. Same nose and mouth. But a different face altogether.

His new face was the one looking at Tim. He was fumbling with his paper milk carton, trying to get it open. It was the square kind where you had to peel apart the outside of one side, then finagle a pie-shaped opening to drink out of by squeezing the two ends until the middle popped up. Honestly, half the time I failed to master the thing, and ended up with cardboard.

Ring was having the same trouble, but his face didn't show it at all. He paused his work on the milk carton and looked directly at Tim. "I know what yuh mean. One time I knew this guy with cewebwal pawsy who used to be a jewk. So I beat the mess out of the kid an' that made me feew a wot bettuh."

He never smiled, but he certainly wasn't frowning. It was more a humorous smugness that knew he had just rattled the cage of the conversation, but he was playing it cool. He went back to fiddling with the milk carton as if nothing had happened.

Tim's eyes grew as big as the Salisbury steak patty on his plate. A short silence ensued and then we all broke into hysterical laughter. Tim shook his head up and down as he laughed and then shoveled a loaded fork of mashed potatoes into his mouth. "Okay, Ring, I hear ya. If I see that kid again, I'll tell him to watch out for you for sure." His mouth was full as he said it, which meant something in the relationship had changed. We would never speak with food in our mouths to people we didn't know. It was a sign of familiarity, especially among teenage guys.

When we got up to leave that lunch, two things stuck out to me as significant: Ring's tray had been untouched, except for his milk carton, and where three friends had walked into a cafeteria one day—they left as four.

16

July 1968

"No more water, please. Everything makes me sick."

Leron could barely whisper the words. She had been vomiting everything up for days now. Her skin was pale. Her once thick and vibrant brown hair had thinned out and become brittle.

The cancer had done its worst, and her best was not good enough to stave it off. It was finishing its terrible work. The end was near.

But so was her victory. She was not dying the desperate woman she had been a few months before. She had walked out of that little country church a changed woman. She had lost her need to blame Oscar or God or fate or anything else. She had gone home whole.

It was not that she never cried. She almost never stopped. She could have harvested her tears by the bucketful. But in her heart she felt tears from someone so much greater. She was no longer crying alone. There was someone to listen. To comfort. To help.

Yet for some strange reason, he was not healing her—at least not in body. She desperately wanted to live, mainly because her David needed her so much. But somewhere along the way, she knew it was coming. And soon. This broke her heart, but it didn't poison it. She had been brought back from the brink into the light—and even in her suffering, she had no desire to live inside the darkness that had dominated her life for so many years. Though she had lived those days cancer-free, there was not even a fraction of the real life in her then that there was now when her body was deteriorating.

Her body was withering, but her spirit had never been healthier.

What else could she do but pray? And now she did. "God, please spare me for David's sake. You know how much help he needs. He needs his momma. Please, God."

It seemed that her prayers were right. They had to be right. The loving God she had come to re-embrace would share her sentiments and spare her family the greatest loss imaginable.

But when peace came into her heart, she found a way to accept her destiny. After all, she truly believed that her life—and her children's lives—were only temporary. Like the Bible said, they were no more than vapors. And whether or not that passing mist lasted sixty years or a hundred and sixty, it was still so brief. She knew that her last breath here was not truly her last—not by a long shot.

The end drew closer. She called her little boy—not nearly so little any more—to her side. She reached up and gently stroked his hair, softly combing down his cowlick with her fingers. Then she pulled his head to her chest. "Oh, my baby boy. I'm so sorry. I wanted to stay with you forever."

"Momma? Pwease stay with meh."

She wept over him, finding a physical energy in her sorrow she had not known for weeks. "Baby, it's not up to me. Oh, I wish it were. I want to stay, but they are calling me home. They are calling me. It's not up to me, baby."

"Is it up to God, Momma?"

She couldn't answer him. She didn't know what to say. Instead she just held her baby close to her breast, where he belonged. And she rocked him gently, which took all the strength she had. He wept too, and she consoled him gently. "Shhh, darling—it's okay. Momma's here, baby. Momma's right here."

But that only made him cry harder. They both knew she would not be there much longer. Finally he settled and she began humming a tune, "Oh, How I Love Jesus." He didn't know the words, but still there was a comfort that cascaded over him for just a moment. One moment—maybe his last with his momma before the end would come. They lay there soaking in it.

Like warm oil, it tingled down his spine.

Then she began coughing again and the nurse pulled him away to tend to her. He was told to leave the room. He didn't want to. He would rather do anything in the world but leave her. Though the sorrow was great here with his momma, he knew what lay beyond that door was worse. At least in here he could still hear her voice. Feel her touch. And though the smell of impending death hung heavy in the air, her perfume still lightened the load.

Out there beyond that door, the dread would surely overtake him again, and envelop him in the cruel arms of the unknown.

The nurse was getting Leron ready to return to the hospital. Between May and October of 1968, she would move back and forth between home and hospital four times, never stabilizing quite enough to remain at home.

The nurse closed the door on him and he stood with his arms crossed in the dark hallway. Alone. He had lost the strength to sob. His stomach was too tightly wound—he had been dry-heaving so much. He wasn't old enough to vocalize all the questions facing him at the moment, yet he felt their weight. Their magnitude. They were unbearable—like an anvil being lowered onto the shoulders of a child. And one with special needs at that.

It was only about 1:30 in the afternoon, but a thick ceiling of dark clouds covered the canopy of the sky. It had rained off and on for days. Inside their old ranch house, the inner hallways were eerily dim. The light coming from the bedrooms was not enough to make much of a difference, and no one turned on the hallway light—the bulbs had burned out a few weeks before and hadn't seemed worth replacing.

David slowly walked down the hallway barefoot, feeling both the softness of the brown shag carpet between his toes as well as the not-so-occasional piece of debris sticking to the bottoms of his feet. No one had vacuumed in a while either. They knew they were coming apart at the seams, but some rips can't be mended. Momma was dying.

That was their lot, and his older brothers and sisters had already begun the process of moving forward without her, at least in their hearts. They knew they had no other choice. But not him. Momma had taught him about God. About hope. About the bond of a family that could never be broken. Even though his daddy had died. Even though he was stuck in this condition.

With all these even-thoughs, he still had but one reality in which to live: hope. And even though the source of that hope was wasting away in the room at the end of the hallway, as long as she was breathing he still lived inside that place of comfort.

David had noticed the change in his mother's spirit after she came home from the church, even though she was dying. That night, she had snatched him up in her arms and held him so close, crying and praying gentle "I'm sorrys" and "thank-yous" as they rocked. A certain odd warmth, like a soft winter blanket, seemed to come from her arms that night as she prayed over him, leaving him more peaceful than he had ever felt in his whole life.

It was a feeling he would often long for and would not feel again for a long time.

After her surgery, she used her remaining time with him to plant seeds in his heart. Seeds of hope. Seeds of love. "David, my darling, you are never alone. You are always loved and cared for, no matter what happens."

In his mind, she was telling him she would never leave. It was a vow he had no reason not to believe. No ability not to believe. Her arms were the only home he had ever known—the only shelter from the raging winds of a world that would never accept him as he was. She was the rock he had hidden under, as well as the rock he would someday build his adult life upon.

Seeing her waste away did not just feel painful; it felt like betrayal. The smashing of a support that was supposed to be a forever thing. The breaking of a promise as strong as gravity's pull or the daily glare of the sunrise. He could not be like his siblings. He could not even try to begin to move on—not because he had nowhere to move, but because her days with him were the very legs upon which he walked. Her heart the very house in which he resided.

And now she was burning down before his very eyes, just as the house they were in had done the year before. It was a cold January morning and Leron had woken up to start a fire in the pot-bellied stove in their living room as she had always done. She went into the kitchen to start breakfast. When she returned to put more wood on the fire, she looked up to see the ceiling engulfed in flames.

She only had time to wake the family and get them outside to safety. The house was made of pine and it burned to the ground in less than an hour. When the school bus pulled up to pick the kids up for school, they were still standing there shivering in their underwear, watching their house burn. It was a total loss.

But Leron would never stay down. She took it upon herself to not only hire men to rebuild it but also to join them in the construction and personally oversee the process. It took a year of hard, stressful work, but she literally helped rebuild their house with her own bare hands.

David wished he could rebuild her health like it was so many beams and rafters, but he didn't have the power. He stood in the hallway and looked up at the walls, lined with lime-green wallpaper dancing with swirling designs and texture. It was supposed to make things brighter, but instead it was an eyesore, clashing with the carpet and his soul. He began slowly walking. There were no pictures of his family hanging on the hallway walls like in most homes—the fire had spared nothing.

Well, actually there was one picture. It was a drawing of Jesus. White robe. Blue sash. Sandy brown hair. Blue eyes.

A Jesus from Missouri rather than the Middle East, though folks didn't fuss over such things in those days.

Momma had told David that God was listening to him. Oh, how she told him, over and over again. She had read to him from the same tattered, leather-bound Bible every night. He remembered the stories of Daniel believing God and laying his head on the soft manes of vicious lions, sleeping like a baby the whole night through.

He remembered David—for she often told him the story of the hero for whom he was named. Gentle and caring yet strong and brave. David with the slingshot, charging at the giant, yet also returning to a place of contrition when he failed on other occasions. A shepherd and a king—and a man after God's own heart. Oh, how she had bathed him in the stories of David, for to her that name was more than a marker, it was a prayer for his future. A prayer for courage in the face of giants. Giants he was too young to be shown, but whose raspy, cruel taunting he was beginning to hear in the distance.

And he remembered Jesus. How could he forget? She was constantly talking to Jesus, and David could tell he answered her. She showed him that Jesus was someone who looked for those whom others passed on the street. Lepers no one else would even come close to. Blind men crying out for help while being told by the crowds to shut their mouths. Children being shooed away even by the disciples. Short guys who climbed trees just to see him because everyone else seemed to have the best view.

David always liked that little guy, Zacchaeus. That story really spoke to him—plus he loved the idea of climbing trees. It was something he wanted so badly to do, but was unable.

Through Momma's sweet and secure voice, all the stories about Jesus had taught him one thing: this man never just walked by without stopping to help. He cared. He listened. He healed.

The darkness seemed to spill downward and pushed him to his knees on the dirty floor. There he put his face on the carpet and whispered, "Pwease, God. Pwease don' take my momma."

He prayed to those heavens, but they never opened for him except to pour more rain. Thunder resonated somewhere, miles away, rolling gently and reminding him that the storm was so vast he could not see the end of it. Still he kept begging.

"Don' take Momma. Pwease don' take Momma."

He lay there for what seemed like hours, but it was only minutes. Frozen moments in the middle of hell. Tears and snot dripped and seeped into the brown fibers beneath his nose. He was a mess. Facedown in the hall. Crushed by the darkness.

A light suddenly broke into the hallway as the bathroom door opened. It was Debbie. The last time her Dan had beaten her, he put her in the hospital for three days. In those days, no one from the medical staff—especially in Montgomery, Alabama, where they had moved after their wedding—thought it serious enough to report. Debbie wasn't surprised—no one had reported it when she was a little girl and her father did the same. And worse.

When she was discharged from the hospital, she never went home to him. She knew he would come looking for her, so she packed her bags and hopped on a Greyhound bus, heading up I-65 North. She had only enough money to get to Nashville. Hopefully that was far enough to avoid another beating.

She borrowed some money from a lady on the bus and called the one and only friend she could think of. Her best friend from junior high and high school—Loretta.

When the call came, Loretta had to break the news to her that Leron, who had been like a mom to both of them, was on her deathbed. It was not convenient, but these situations never are. Loretta insisted that instead of coming to Liberty, Debbie should head west through Memphis and meet her at Leron's house in Jonesboro.

After all, Leron would love to see Debbie before the end came. So in addition to the circumstances of their family's darkest hour, they also had a houseguest. She was coming out of the bathroom after taking a shower. She wore a pink bathrobe with a matching pink satin belt tied in a bow around her waist. Her hair was wrapped up in a white towel on her head. She looked to her left and saw David lying there.

"David?" She lifted him to his feet and pulled him close to her chest. "It's okay. It's going to be okay."

"Aw yuh shuwah?" He sniffled. He had met Debbie several times when he was much younger. She was a grown woman, like his sister, but much nicer to him. Her concern was comforting.

"Of course I'm sure! We're going to take care of you no matter what happens." Everyone knew it wouldn't be much longer for Leron. Debbie took hold of his hand, interlocking their fingers. "Come with me, let's get you cleaned up. You're a mess." They walked down the hallway and into Loretta's room. She was gone to the store to buy more food to make dinner.

He walked in and sat on the bed as she closed the door behind them. The calm and comforting demeanor she had been showing David faded, but he was staring at the floor and didn't notice.

It was not a fake mask that she took off. It was more of a second face—one she herself didn't even know she had. Both faces were real, but the one now revealing itself was unstable, to say the least. The responsible woman in her midtwenties quickly morphed into someone else. She felt like it was her momma too who lay dying in the next room. She was wrought with grief, for many reasons.

But there was something else there. Something damaged. A hidden wound from many years ago that no one, probably not even Loretta, knew about. It had been inflicted violently upon her at a tender age, leaving scars unseen and always fresh. Always bleeding somewhere deep inside. Always hiding what she wished would have killed her. Instead she carried a death that never let her die.

No one else knew whose hands had wounded her—touched her in a way she should have never been touched at that age. No one would ever know—could ever know. The secret was embedded in her heart like a poison dart. It had become one with her, covered and hidden. There was no reaching her at those depths, but the evidence of her past destruction would forever leak out and poison those around her.

She was not the person Loretta knew, not at that moment anyway. The monster in her past somehow lived within her now. Took over sometimes. Made her do things. And as the years had passed, it became harder and harder to know where she ended and it began.

There had been a time when she felt herself hanging on to a ledge, high above the blackness. She had been suspended there for so long and now, in the pain and the grief, she just couldn't hang on and she gave herself over to the darkness. Let herself fall into it.

Only dimly conscious of such feelings, she walked over to David and sat down beside him on the bed. She pulled some tissues out of the small square box on the nightstand and began wiping his face and helping him blow his nose. Just as his momma or sister would have done, even though he had never been that close to Loretta.

Even so, there was something non-maternal about her touch. Her hand lingered too long upon his shoulder. Her fingers worked too long through his hair. Unlike the comfort of his mother's touch that tingled down his spine, hers sent shivers instead.

As a fourteen-year-old boy in the midst of such pain and mourning, he found her caresses strange and confusing. He wasn't sure what was right or what to feel. No one had ever brought forward such raw feelings in him—private, sensual feelings—and for a moment he felt deep shame. Thoughts and responses like his, in such times as these, were too horrible to entertain even for a moment. Even wrapped in grief, he knew something was wrong.

She seemed to sense his hesitancy and upped the manipulation of his fragile frame of mind. "It's okay, baby. Your momma wants me to be here for you. This is what she wants."

David had no idea how the world worked, and she was not about to tell him. Besides, he had no one else left to trust. No one else left to listen to. Debbie knew this. She understood that she could get whatever she wanted.

And with his kind and motherly caretaker dying in the room next door, she stood up and took the towel from her hair, shaking it out and then rubbing her fingers through it.

David looked up at her through innocent, tear-filled eyes, feeling tortured that she had his attention like she did. He had no idea what was going on, and thus he did not have the ability to leave.

Then she slowly began untying the satin belt around her waist.

17

Summer 1970

Our junior year, with all its mastery of the art of adolescence, quickly came to an end. Almost—but not quite—reluctantly, we plunged headlong into summer vacation. The very best of high school still can't compete with the glory of any ordinary summer.

Time seemed to fly—as happens, they say, when you're having fun. I guess sometimes clichés were actually coined for legitimate reasons. In the midst of all the fun with Ring and the boys, everything in my own life seemed to accelerate too.

During those times, my friends were always right beside me and I knew it was a season of life that would never again return. We were alive—in every sense of the word. Breathing freely. Drinking deeply of the small-town high school experience and all it had to offer us—and it was an experience unlike any other.

Liberty was our semi-adult playground and it offered us a town large enough for enjoyment but small enough for safety. The days were long and full of sunshine, and the nights were filled with cool breezes and even cooler sodas as we would hang out with dozens of friends—girls included—down at Begg's.

That was the year I finally got my first car too. A 1969 Dodge Coronet. It was not the Mustang of my dreams, but I never felt even a single ounce of regret or a solitary reason to complain. It was *my* car. The car. Any car. The ultimate symbol of teenage freedom. It meant I was now the captain of a vessel all my own. I could steer it anywhere I wished, and with the slightest push of my foot it would obey.

My car was to me a bestowing of power—good power, not the bad kind that lands some teenage boys in the county lock-up for stupid things like egging houses or snatching car radios. My car was my piece of an American rite of passage, signaling to all that a boy had become trustworthy enough to be about his own business. In a time when plenty of older guys who had graduated from our school were being drafted and shipped off to the jungles of Vietnam, I guess all of us boys on the cusp of manhood felt a certain need to grow up as quickly as possible.

No one really knew exactly how long life might last, which I suppose was always true. But it seemed so much truer when the military sedan pulled up to a family's house and those decorated officers in their dress blues approached someone's front door. Usually, the poor mother inside had already seen them through the window and was already collapsed in grief on the floor before they could even break the news. Another young man killed in action. Another momma outliving her babies.

Our generation was being thinned out by a war we didn't understand and of which we could see no end. We knew that guys our age were being entrusted with machine guns and rocket launchers, so we felt the need to get as much power in our hands as possible. It was not a time to be weak. We needed to feel the power and know that we could control it. To steer it without crashing. To let it take us places bigger than Liberty, even if we rarely ever drove to those places. That mobile hunk of steel, rubber, and chrome represented sheer possibility—to us it seemed nothing short of a sign that we could do anything.

But mostly, we used our cars for cruising. We would begin at Kuku and then head over to the new Dairy Queen that had just opened for business. The point of stopping at one or the other was not to actually order something. It was to see who was there. We would spend an hour or so heading between the two until we had filled up our cars.

My passenger manifest would vary a bit, but it almost always included two copilots, Jeff and Ring. Tim would also ride with us a lot, but he also ran with another group of friends. Plus, he usually had a girlfriend—meaning, over the course of time, he had many girlfriends—who kept him occupied. But Jeff and Ring were always with me, along with whomever else we could fit into the Dodge.

Once our vehicles were full, we would head out to cruise the triangle. The three points in this triangle were the Kuku, the city park, and the baseball park. Our church was right across the street from the city park. The line of cars wasn't much to write home about, but to us, it seemed as if the whole world would come together to have fun. We didn't worry about seat belts or speed limits. We drove slowly on purpose so we could see all the other cruisers and be able to talk to them through our car windows.

We cruised our way through the summer and it cruised its way to Labor Day, as summer vacations always do. You come to the end of it and realize that your life is about to take an ominous step forward—a new grade, a higher stage in the pecking order of life. And when it happens to be your senior year, you realize that the last of your childhood has all but drained away. You've come of age.

We returned to campus like conquering heroes. It was now that Ring truly went from outcast to broadcast. That face I had first seen in the darkness of his basement had been transformed by the light that lit up the orange carpet in my dad's church. He talked to everyone he saw. Everywhere he saw them. He paraded through the school hallways with the joy of Santa Claus with a bag full of presents, except his gifts were smiles and "Heys!"

He became a tangible connection point for the student body. Like something they all touched every day for good luck, though not in a dismissive or patronizing way. He wasn't their rabbit's foot or four-leaf clover. He was their pick-me-up—and he was the initiator of the picking up process. He became the person who was the first to greet you in the morning and the last to greet you as you walked out the door. And if you hadn't seen any smiles for an entire day, just find Ring; he never ran out. His pleasantness never seemed to dissipate. He became a guy who was just that happy that often.

So as he walked down the hall, voices would call left and right. "Ring!" To which he would reply with "Hey!" So the "Heys!" and "Rings!" flew about out like popcorn audibly coming to temperature in a tinfoil pan on a hot stove. You never knew when they were going to pop, but they would, and they did so often. Hands were extended as he passed by, patting him on the back or shaking his outstretched hand.

We knew everybody and everybody knew us. Tim had completed a great junior season as the starting quarterback and was gearing up for his senior year. He told us that during summer workouts, Ring started showing up at every practice—even two-a-days. There was a black five-gallon bucket left behind the field house that a contractor had used for mixing concrete when he put in the new sidewalk. Ring would retrieve that bucket and turn it over to make himself a little seat on the sidelines.

At first, it wasn't clear whether or not Coach Hall was going to let him stay there. He would make him scoot his bucket back away from the sidelines. "Quit crowding the field, Ring. You're going to get killed out here."

Ring would just look at him and smile.

"Yes, suh." And then he would move his bucket back a few yards. Coach H, as we called him, would then stand in front of him in that exact spot on the sidelines, blowing his whistle and yelling at the players. It seemed as if he had determined that wherever Ring was going to sit on his bucket, that was the exact place he needed to stand.

But every time he got on Ring about it, all he heard in return was a kind and gentle, "Yes, suh."

Coach H was not one of those coaches who actually believed all the drill sergeant stuff he spewed at his players. It was a role he played in order to keep control. But when it wasn't practice or game time, he was actually a very funny guy, joking around with his students and players, poking fun—especially with the upperclassmen.

The basketball players would sometimes join the football players during the summer for weight lifting. One day that summer, we were joking around with Coach H in the weight room when the subject of Ring came up.

"Boys, I see you three hanging out with Ring at school. I've got to know: What's the deal with him and that bucket?"

We all laughed, but not in a mean way. You didn't have to be making fun of him to admit that Ring sitting on that black bucket was an amusing sight to behold.

Tim spoke up. "Yeah, Ring is hilarious. You would like him, Coach."

Coach H opened his eyes real wide for a second, as if he was surprised by the words, but didn't want to show it. "Well, that's a little surprising to hear, for sure. From what I heard last year about him, 'hilarious' was not the word I would have expected."

Jeff piped in this time. "He's changed, Coach H. He really has. You should try talking to him sometime."

Coach H had started picking up dirty paper towels and other trash from the concrete floor and throwing them into the can while we were talking. "Hmm. Maybe I will sometime."

The floor was littered with athletic tape, face masks, and other miscellaneous junk that magically appeared after every practice—and equally as magically, never seemed to come from any of the players. Phantom trash. Every time Coach H would get on the players about it, every guy maintained his innocence.

Coach kept right on cleaning as he was thinking. All the work he was doing gave me an idea.

"Coach H, do you clean up in here every day?"

"You mean, do I act like a mommy to all you little girls who can't seem to keep your garbage off the floor around here? I guess I do, Wideman. I guess I do." Then he threw a filthy towel in my face. We all laughed—and I almost gagged too.

"That's a shame, Coach. You really should get somebody else to do this kind of thing. You're the head coach, for crying out loud! You've got bigger and better things to do than pick up Jeff's jockstrap!" We all knew that at a school our size, the head coaching position was really not that huge a deal. Coach H knew this too, but he was more than okay with it. Small-town living was not a bad thing at all. Still, he played along with me.

"You volunteering, Wideman? I'm not sure you got what it takes."

I chuckled a bit and said, "No sir, I'm a little busy for that. But I think I know someone who would work—and who would love to do it."

"Who?"

"Ring."

The other guys picked up on my plan and added their glowing endorsements. Five minutes later, David Ring was the new manager of the Liberty High School football program. We took him out to Kuku to celebrate, but as always, he didn't eat anything. Only his soda cup was empty when the night was over.

After that, I'm here to tell you the boy never seemed to go home. He was early to every football practice and stayed late for cleanup. He was the best manager Liberty had ever seen. He was also the most celebrated.

When the season finally started, which was usually a week or two before school actually began, Ring was sitting on the bus right alongside the rest of the guys. He joined in the team cheers. He paced the sidelines beside Coach Hall, doing anything and everything he asked. You could tell that Coach had taken quite a liking to him. This became most clear during the first pep rally of the year.

Football pep rallies were pretty predicable. After the cheerleaders would go through all their "rah rahs," the crowd would muster up the best noise it could make. Then Coach H would announce each of the players as they entered from the door that led from the cafeteria to the gym.

Most of the players weren't crazy about this tradition, because some guys would get a lot more crowd response than others. Besides, who could really hear anything for the crazy echoes in that old gym anyway? Voices sounded a lot like Charlie Brown's teacher from the *Peanuts* cartoon.

That day, this roll call ended, as usual, with the name of the second string right tackle, Jesse Zilham. Due to his family roots and good old ABC order, he was always the last and most embarrassed player to run out there. That's when Principal Davenport usually took the microphone and went into his spiel.

But not today. The coach said into the mike, "And last, but certainly not least, I think you should all get up on your feet and give a warm Bluejays welcome to the newest addition to our team. Team manager David Ring!"

When Ring's name was called, the gym came to life in a way I had never heard it. Ring emerged from the doorway wearing a blue jersey with a yellow double zero printed across the chest. It might as well have been a huge red S, complete with cape and outside-the-clothes underwear. He held on with all of his might to a huge blue and yellow flag bearing the initials LHS.

The applause was loaded with whistles and cheers, as if Julius Caesar himself was riding in a chariot through the rose-laden streets of Rome after conquering Gaul.

When he heard the students cheering and chanting his name, his face lit up like the night sky on the Fourth of July.

He continued in his version of jogging, as fast as he could, while the accolades continued to pour down upon him. When he finally reached the rest of the team, in an impromptu display of camaraderie, the whole crew broke their ranks and came together, jumping around in a little huddle of energy. And who was right in the middle of their ring? Ring.

It was the best pep rally we ever had, before or since. And from that day forward, David Ring's place at the center of life in Liberty was forever solidified. I couldn't believe what I was seeing.

Something else did catch my eye though. It was Ms. Myers leaning against the wall. The expression on her face was intriguing, to say the least. She looked happy and excited, as all the faculty and students seemed to be, but beyond that she seemed fascinated—even awestruck—by the scene. For her, this was an equation that didn't balance out.

We made brief eye contact. She smiled and nodded her head. I guess she finally believed what Ring had said about us being friends.

If students were fond of Ring before the pep rally, they loved the guy afterward. For that matter, girls loved him. And he loved them right back. He was constantly a magnet for the prettiest girls in the school, receiving huge hugs by the dozens. Cheerleaders. Volleyball players. Even the student council types. Ring was never lacking in female affection. We used to give him quite the hard time for being such a "ladies' man."

He would laugh, but I always noticed that he was just a little uncomfortable about responding to the opposite sex. He returned affection in controlled doses. It was almost as if he hadn't quite come to terms with girls and their place in his world. He was kind and accepting—or, with us, funny and sarcastic—but there was definitely something in him that was a little off-kilter when it came to women. I chalked it up to embarrassment and inexperience. Hey, all guys went through that. I know I did.

So we figured Ring would get the hang of the girl thing sooner or later. At the rate he was going, he'd be running for mayor at some point. He was picking up fans right and left—among them my parents, who constantly doted on him. Later on that school year, they would come to cheer him on in basketball, along with their own son.

Yes, David Ring turned out to be such a great football manager that Coach H suggested him for "hoops" season as well—more fodder for Ring's busy social calendar. It seemed as if he never went home after school. There was always a game. Always a practice. Always a team meeting that required his attendance. Or so he insisted.

The team would run through a huge paper banner, held by the cheerleaders, before games. Ring was called upon to lead the team in that run. The crowd would erupt as that young man with cerebral palsy broke through that banner with a smile as wide as Missouri and a team that loved him. He was living the dream.

It made our team unique in two ways. One, our manager led the charge. Two, it gave us the slowest "triumphal entry" of any school in the district. Slow but fun—we loved every minute of it.

The school community was not the only one to surround him. Our church stayed true to their unspoken vow from the altar. Being Protestant, we didn't have altar boys, but he was our version of that tradition. He became my Dad's shadow. Again, he was kind of over-the-top in his attention to helping, always showing up early to pitch in. At every potluck dinner, he was patted on the head and doted on by every sweet little old lady within a hundred-foot radius.

Our youth group celebrated him in much the same way. We were always at ice cream socials or pizza socials or soda socials, and Ring was pretty much at the center of anything we did that was social.

But when there was nothing especially social going on, he was usually at our house. He would eat with us, even on Sundays after church. He no longer qualified as a guest at our dinner table; he was as much a part of the family as anyone else. He had his own chair and his own place in the family circle.

I even found out why his plate stayed full up to the end of meals. His speech and eating were both so belabored that he was embarrassed trying to do both in front of people. He was afraid others wouldn't like seeing what he went through. But as time passed, he made an exception for us. We didn't stare at him, and we learned the patient rhythm of talking with him between bites. You didn't ask him a question if his mouth was full. Basically, we did what any family would do—we adapted for our little brother. And I think that meant something to him.

One night, my grandma was eating dinner with us. Because of her age, her hands would shake pretty severely. Ring asked her which one of them she thought would spill a drink first. No more than thirty seconds later, he knocked over his glass of tea and the whole table exploded into laughter.

A family kind of laughter.

Sometimes I sat back, took a good look at Ring, and felt the amazement all over again. How could a person change so drastically, so quickly?

This was a big deal for me. It planted within me something like real faith in the idea of transformation. God could really change somebody from the inside out. It validated what I believed. It reassured me that this church thing—my family's work in this town, in this life—was not worthless.

Of course, I didn't fully make all these connections at the time, but nevertheless some inner part of me was galvanized. What I believed about God and people and family and never giving up on someone in need—these things could actually work. They weren't just ideas, or thoughts on some stuffy guy's chalkboard or feltboard. This was the big stuff for which little preachers in little churches did little works to keep getting a little paycheck.

Ring's transformation was proof to me. Proof of what, only time would tell. There were plenty of moments to come in my life when hard evidence would be needed in the courtroom of my circumstances. Moments of doubt. Pain. Questions. Fears. When I stood on the stand in those moments, I would always remember Ring and 1970. There was the proof I needed. Proof that anything was possible. Proof that anyone could change.

I knew I was in the middle of one of those "golden years" of growing up—the best part of being a teenager. And the "golden year" of 1970 may not have been so shiny without the gold Ring. Who knows? I felt sure we were living more than a high school dream; we were living a dream, period—one that few people ever get to experience. Rarely in life, especially early on, do we get to find such incredible joy in someone else's good fortune.

The closest high school experience I can think of is being a member of a sports team. Some kid becomes the hero of the big game, and you're as happy for him as he is for himself. But this was deeper than football trophies. I found myself watching Ring walk down the hallway, greeting everyone and slapping backs. And I was overjoyed, even though it wasn't about me in any tangible way. I was able to experience what it meant to get purely unselfish pleasure from someone else's victories.

That year of 1970 changed me forever. It caused me to embrace new confidence in myself and in what was to come. It calibrated something in me to try for more. To reach higher. To live up to the level of hope I had seen brought back from the dead in him.

18

October 1968

Leron died in October 1968. She left the world from Saint Bernard's Medical Center, the same place where David had entered it.

After her death, J. D., her second husband, showed that he was nothing if not consistent. In the past, he had cheated with Leron while she was another man's wife. Now, as Leron lay dying, he had an affair with her nurse. Once the funeral was over, he married that nurse and moved her into the very house Leron had rebuilt with her two hands and fighting spirit.

Leron had fought the good fight until the last round. But when she left, David gave up the battle. He was a boy with no land to fight for. No place to call home. No commander to give him direction.

Since Debbie was seemingly glued to Loretta's side, her strange and unwanted advances continued. Debbie was at the funeral as if she was one of the family. Still, her actions weren't merely an oddity of a suffering home in the throes of grief. David couldn't understand what they were, but at least there had been temporary deliverance when his oldest sister, Bernice, stepped forward to take him once it was clear to everyone that Leron was not going to recover. Bernice's family lived in St. Charles, Missouri. In July 1968, several months before his mother died, he moved there to get settled in before school started in September. It was there shortly after that he heard the news his momma was gone from this earth.

The storms didn't clear away but only seemed to multiply in his family. David was bullied mercilessly at the local school in St. Charles. Not that he noticed much, really. His grief was so deep, so absolute. The hole left inside him, once filled by his mother, was too gaping. Too painful. Everything else was background noise.

It was now that he declared war on life itself. He became bitter at the lack of any goal worth living for. So he simply stopped living.

The bullies did not take notice of his pain. He was laughed at. Mocked. Mimicked. Even knocked down more than once. No one seemed to care, so neither did he. On the other hand, he chose not to continue facing the giants at school. Without his momma there to advocate and defend him, he was not the David she had proclaimed him to be. No Goliaths were going to fall by his sling. Her Bible story was just that—a story.

He was done.

That's when he stopped going to school. His sister would drop him off at the bus stop, but once her car had disappeared over the horizon as she headed on to work, he would simply walk back to their house.

His grades plummeted, as did his relationship with those who had taken him in. In the best of circumstances his special needs were a burden. But who needed a teenage dropout? Who needed a perpetually angry face at the dinner table? In time, they would inevitably throw their hands in the air and give up. Let someone else take a shot at caring for this boy.

Someone like Bonnie, yet another sister, and her husband, Buddy. They tried their best, but with the little brother came the big black cloud. It was six months before life became too complicated in this new household. They were already facing multiple crises of their own, and David's presence was one crisis over the limit.

Phone calls were made. Suitcases were packed.

But the end of the line was closing in. One of his brothers had a thought—maybe this little brother should really be in an orphanage. That was the island for misfit toys, the place for special needs when the needs became too—special.

There was only one sibling between David and that destination: Loretta.

He found himself bound for Liberty, Missouri.

Loretta agreed to take him, thus he was sent to her house—and to the discovery that there were levels of suffering he hadn't yet plumbed. Punishments that seemed unrelated to his behavior. Confusion he'd thought he'd left behind forever.

For many months, he listened for the soft footsteps of his older sister's best friend, stealing through the darkness down to his basement room.

19

August 1970

Debbie paced back and forth, smoking a cigarette in the dark.

Rod was working third shift again. Loretta and the kids were asleep. Her eyes were moving about wildly, unable to focus on one thing at a time. It was one of her manic moments.

She walked down the steps to the basement—into David's room. She leaned against the wall, staring at the empty bed, neatly made. The blanket and linens were without wrinkle or crease.

She looked at the clock. It was past 2:30 in the morning and David still wasn't home. She knew why he'd been coming home so late. It was just his way of dodging her.

She sighed heavily as she leaned against the wall. He was out there somewhere—what was he doing? What could he be saying to people? When would he come home?

She could feel something warm on her left thumb, just beside her thumbnail. She had been unconsciously scratching at it again, bringing a little blood. Sign of nerves.

She took a long drag on the cigarette and blew the smoke into the empty room. Empty woman in an empty room.

And then she heard something—a faint creaking. A door being pushed open ever so slowly.

Ring hated his basement room, but it did have one advantage. He could avoid the front door, coming and going with maximum stealth. The kitchen was adjacent to the garage, so all he had to do was open the big garage door manually and slip in.

Since that night at church—that night when everything in life had changed for him—he had used every excuse he could imagine to stay away from the house and Debbie. He had to sleep there, so he just made sure he came home at all hours of the night. And once he was in, he would lock the door to the upstairs steps. What a feeling of security that brought him.

Tonight, for some reason, the garage door wouldn't budge. He would have to find some other way in. It was yet another moment—as if he needed any more—of finding something his cerebral palsy wouldn't let him do. There was no way he could sneak through the living room window and slip from there into the kitchen to the door leading into the basement. That way he could have bypassed the main hallway connected to her bedroom, as well as the huge front door. That door creaked like the coffin from the Dracula movie he'd seen at Tim's house a few weeks before.

He considered the window just the same, pushing himself awkwardly past the overgrown branches of the holly bush in front of the window. But his fingers just couldn't manage to work the window open, and the scratches and scrapes were accumulating like little red checkmarks all over his arms and the tops of his hands. He stepped back onto the cracked driveway and stared at the front door.

The moon hung high in the night sky, shining about three-quarters full and offering ample light to see the front porch. But nevertheless, he knew darkness was behind that door—the door he had no choice but to enter. He'd brought along a little orange flashlight; he'd borrowed it from a friend for these late-night prowls outside the house.

His key unlocked the dead bolt on the front door, and he began inching the door open with the speed of a wounded snail, hoping not to awaken the person he wanted least in the world to see right now. To his chagrin, Rod had still not oiled the hinges. The creaking seemed to him to be louder than a twenty-one-gun salute, and he just knew she would wake up. He figured out that slowly opening the door ultimately made more racket, so he hurried it the rest of the way open and stood there gazing down the hallway for a moment, listening.

He removed his shoes, then looked at his watch. It was 2:37 a.m.—not an uncommon time for him to come home. All the lights in the house were off, save one small yellow bulb over the oven. Pots and pans were piled high on the inactive burners. They made jagged shadows on the opposite wall, reminding him of soldiers carrying various weapons of war. A familiar shiver made its way up and down David's spine.

By the looks of it, no one had washed any dishes in days. Several flies delightfully buzzed around the endless bounty of food particles and crumbs left for them all over the counters and in the sink. It was disgusting. All of it. And Ring momentarily took note of the differences between the Wideman home and this one. He realized this place felt nothing like home. It never had, even though he lived here.

It wasn't just the lack of tidiness. There was an atmosphere. An ethos of shadows. An uneasiness he felt grow with each step he took across the filthy carpet beneath his stocking feet. He was already a slow mover, but combined with his attempts to be quiet, it took him more than seven minutes to balance himself and span a distance that would normally take only a few seconds.

All in all, he managed to move through the kitchen with more stealth than he thought he possessed. He could hear little breaths and big snores echoing from the kids' rooms. Their small collective noises provided him just the cover he needed, because, after all, Debbie's room was at the end of the hallway, just past theirs.

He finally reached the door to the basement and opened it slowly. Silently. He knew better than to turn on the lights to see the steps. He didn't need to. He was no stranger to being without light in this part of the house. Plus he had his flashlight. He tiptoed down the first two steps and then gently closed the door behind him. Then he was free to walk more normally, so to speak, down the stairs. Still, he did so slowly and methodically.

And once again, Ring descended into the darkness he had lived in for so long.

He continued to use the flashlight instead of turning on the overhead light, just to keep residual light from escaping into the upstairs. Ring walked over to the chest of drawers and began emptying his pockets. He looked at the various knickknacks he had left on top of it. His shaving cup and shaving brush to lather up the soap, along with the double-edged razor that had been his father's. He'd found it while rummaging through some of his momma's things after she died. There, also, was his old dull pocketknife.

He saw a small ball of rubber bands he had made while sitting in the darkness for hours on end. It gave his idle and slow-moving hands something to do to pass the time. He shined his flashlight on the ball, illuminating the reds, blues, greens, and whites crisscrossing its surface.

He reached down to open a drawer and retrieve a clean shirt to sleep in. As he straightened, his flashlight shone in the mirror above his chest of drawers. That's when he saw her in the reflection.

His heart leapt as he spun around and stumbled backward into the chest of drawers, dropping his flashlight, which clanked on the floor and spun. Debbie was sitting on his bed, where she had been watching him the whole time. The flashlight continued spinning around in slow circles on the concrete, each swoop casting light on her.

He steadied himself as the flashlight came to rest. Its residual light was enough to let them see each other. Her eyes were locked on him, as if she hadn't blinked for hours. Most of her body was hidden by darkness, but the little bit of light made her brown eyes stand out almost as if they were not inside her head at all.

She didn't move. Didn't speak. He couldn't tell if she was angry or upset. What she was at that moment was indiscernible. She was none of the above. All of the above.

Ring noticed that his hands were trembling uncontrollably. He stared a moment, grasping for his composure, before finally stammering, "Debbie! What aw yuh doin' down heuh?"

She tilted her head to the side and then ran her fingers through her hair. "Waiting for you." Her voice was some odd combination of anger and seductiveness.

"But—but how did yuh know when I was comin'?"

"I didn't. But I knew you'd come home sometime—and I knew I would hear you if you couldn't open the garage door." She was doe-eyed, as if her eyes were taped wide open.

"Debbie, I'm not doin' dis anym—"

She exploded. "This is your home, David! And I'm your family!"

She still never blinked, but her left upper eyelid twitched. She stood up and began walking toward him. "You think you can just stop that easy! Momma would be so disappointed in you, David!"

Something in Ring snapped.

"Yuh don' tawk 'bout Momma! Yuh don' say heh name! She's not yo' momma. Dis stops wight now!"

Debbie's eyes began blinking wildly, as if she had never seen anything like this before. *Who was this boy? What had happened to him?* She was on her heels; clearly, she had never expected him to stand up to her. But he had. Finally, he had. He could feel it, a newly grown layer of young manhood, covering his childlike need, giving him new strength.

He squinted his eyes. "Yuh aw not my famiwy! Yuh aw a monstuh!"

He stood there trembling for a moment, deciding what came next. Because now, he realized, that could happen. He could *decide*.

He picked up the flashlight and began his slow walk toward the steps and the light switch.

Debbie ran to him as he was walking away, putting her hand on his shoulder. She began to weep. "You're right, David! I am a monster! I never meant to hurt you."

He paused. He had never heard her talk like this. Ever.

"I don't know how to live here anymore. Dan hurt me real bad, David. I'm broken. I know I am. And it's nice that Loretta lets me live here, but the kids just scream and cry and run around me all day. I can't take it anymore, David! I can't! Please don't leave me—you're the only one I care about!"

He listened carefully, without looking at her. It sounded real—and Ring wasn't sure what to do with that. So many lines had been crossed and blurred so many times. It was impossible for him to discern what was true. He didn't know normal—she had dashed normal against the rocks two years ago. And now he had let a family and God gather around him—and within him—and pick up the pieces of his shattered self.

They had put the pieces back together, believing that those pieces would form a picture that was good. They had believed in him, and he was going to be that good person now, the one they believed in. He was going to care.

It was that determination to care that made him pause. Made him hesitate. Made him listen to her tear-filled ramblings, regardless of what she might deserve. For a moment, he wondered if maybe she could get some help—the way he had. Maybe Brother Don or the folks from the church. Maybe a doctor or a shrink. Maybe—

As he was contemplating these things, she was crying on his shoulder from behind. But then something changed.

She continued to sniffle, but slowly she brought herself fully behind him, pressing her breasts against his back. She then wrapped her arms around him and put her hands on his chest. That old, familiar, terrible shiver chilled its way down his spine. He dropped the flashlight.

Whipping around in a fury, he grabbed hold of her wrists with a physical strength he had never displayed before. His eyes blazed. "No! Yuh wiw nevuh touch me 'gain."

She stared as if he were a ghost, the blood drained from her cheeks. He didn't let go of her wrists, and as he continued squeezing them, she flinched in pain.

And then she was someone else entirely. Ring saw the change.

She leaned toward him, her lips quivering in rage. "I'll have you put into a home! You won't have anywhere to go. No—one—wants—you." She gritted her teeth, huffing with the force of her fury. "You are nothing but a stupid, crippled retard!"

He let go and pushed her away from him as hard as he could. She fell to the ground. He stood over her as she trembled, struggling to catch her breath, and it seemed that, for the first time, she was scared of him instead of the other way around.

He was breathing heavily as well. And he didn't care which version of Debbie he was talking to. He had a message for all of them. He pointed a crooked finger at her and said, in a full and clear tone, "I am not a weetaud! I have a famiwy—and I know God wuvs me. I'm not afwaid of yuh anymoh."

She seemed paralyzed with shock. She sat there on the cold concrete just watching him. He continued. "Yuh stay 'way fwom meh. Owah I pwomise I'll tew evewybody what yuh did to meh. I'll tew my sista. I'll tew Bwotha Don. I towd you, I'm not afwaid anymoh."

Her face became whiter than ever. Almost deathly. She stumbled to her feet and hurried up the stairs. When she got to the top, she paused to look back down at him.

He stared at her with narrowed eyes. Calmly. He said, "Now it's yo' tuwn to be afwaid."

She slammed the door. He slowly began walking up the steps. Halfway up, he reached above his head and yanked the string, turning on the light bulb and leaving it dangling back and forth in the stairwell. No more darkness.

Then he walked back down into his room to go to sleep, but this time he didn't lock the door. His basement room finally had some light—at least for a night.

He needed his sleep; soon the sun would chase away the last of the darkness. And for the first time, he had some idea about the hope of a new day.

20

September 1970

"A Ring Is a Girl's Best Friend!"

It was hard for me to say without laughing. Those passing by got a good chuckle out of the line. "Vote David Ring for vice president," I told them.

I was standing at the door to the hallway where most of the seniors' lockers were located. The sign I was holding had been painted by some of the cheerleaders after school the day before. They were making banners for the baseball field, and they had painted us a good one while they were at it. By this time, Ring had the cheerleaders at his beck and call.

And just about everybody else too. He was a pep rally icon. Ring had pretty much become the school's mascot, head of the student cheering section, and the most celebrated manager in the history of Liberty High School. Maybe of any school.

You might think it was a kind of condescending pat on the back, designed to make us feel good about ourselves. Just the opposite was true—it was all about admiration, feeling good about him.

The Liberty student body had truly come to love David Ring. He had become a constant, uplifting presence around school. He was kind. He was real. And he was always encouraging. And perhaps most of all, he was a reminder that people can change, even in the hardest of circumstances. He made all of us want to reach for something better in our lives.

I guess you could say we weren't just cheering for him. We were cheering for the idea that nothing could hold us down if we set our minds to it. We were on the verge of adulthood, and here was somebody to show us that anything was possible. Talk about a pep rally. We were fired up for a lot more than athletic games.

We were also protective of Ring. This became evident in the district basketball tournament later on, during the spring semester. We were playing one of our rivals—Fort Osage High School from Independence, right across the river. They were anchored by a six-foot-five all-star center named Derrick Rutledge. He was a beast of a man on a court filled with boys. During the game, there had been a foul on Tim, and the two teams lined up across from each other as per usual, Tim waiting at the free-throw line.

"All right, guys, two shots, two shots." The referee stood under the basket and threw a bounce pass to Tim at the line. He did his traditional two dribbles, then spun the ball backward in his hands and paused to shoot. Release.

Follow-through. Swish. Tim had a nearly perfect jump shot and was a 90 percent free-throw shooter.

"One shot, boys. One shot."

Tim began his same pre-shot routine.

"Hey Bennett, try not to miss this one."

It was Rutledge, positioned directly under the right side of the backboard. He was leaning over with his hands on his knees, taking a breather. A smirk was pasted on his face, but Tim didn't even acknowledge he existed. This sort of thing was just a part of the game. Tim was a pillar of focused energy. He dribbled twice and started into his backspin.

Rutledge continued. "Try not to shoot it like your manager over there. Where'd you guys find him? The short bus stop?"

Tim had lettered in three sports during all four years of high school. He had been the starting point guard on the basketball team for the three previous seasons. And this was the first time he had ever stopped his foul shooting routine. He held the ball and looked at Rutledge with a stoic expression. Four other sets of eyes—the other Liberty players—turned in his direction at the same time.

From the sidelines, Coach Stevens, the Liberty basketball coach, couldn't hear what had been said. But he certainly noticed that Tim had broken his shooting stride. And that never happened. He knew something strange was going on, so he initiated a standard coaching move, reassuring him from the sidelines. "Focus! Put it in the hoop, Tim!"

Tim looked over at the coach and saw Ring standing behind the bench. He had a blue towel in his hand, and he was watching the whole scenario play out. Like the coach, he was oblivious to the trash talk.

Tim turned back toward the basket, snapping himself back into game shape. The crowd kept cheering or jeering, depending on which section they sat in.

Tim restarted his foul shot routine. Dribbled twice. Backspin.

"Hey, Bennett, why don't we get that retard out here to get your rebound when you miss?" Rutledge again.

Tim never looked at him. Never even acknowledged that he had said anything at all. He finished his backspin and prepared to shoot—then threw a full-speed chest pass straight down the lane and hit Rutledge squarely in the face. Rutledge went down in a heap, trying to cup the stream of blood flowing from his broken nose.

It was on.

In less than a blink, the lane was a writhing mob of players laying into each other like medieval warriors. Soon the two benches were cleared and punches were being thrown left and right. The coaches and referees scurried about, shouting, yanking jerseys, and forcing themselves between players. It was a melee of whistles and yelling.

Tim looked up from his position prone on the floor. He had apparently taken on someone on the Fort Osage wrestling team, and he was in a death lock. But there was a smile on his face, because he was looking toward the Liberty bench. It was all clear but for one figure.

Ring. He had once been someone to ignore, due to his own rudeness. Now he had become someone to fight for.

Even to vote for.

Back in the fall, when the guys talked him into running for senior class vice president, I naturally volunteered to be his campaign manager.

It was September—an amazing month, looking back. This one had a twist. Class officers and student council officers were usually elected the previous spring, so they could begin leading in the fall as the new school year began. But near the end of our junior year, Mrs. Gaines, the student council faculty sponsor, went on maternity leave. With her absence, the election for the next year's positions got lost in the transition of substitutes and interim teachers.

By the time anyone figured it out, we were already in final exams and there was no time for an election. So Principal Davenport made an announcement that all elections for the next year's officers would be made early in the fall semester. No one knew that over that summer and throughout the fall Ring would become the most popular guy in school.

So when the time for elections rolled around, Ring was the front-runner for senior class vice president. My role as his campaign manager had two goals: getting others to make signs, and getting my parents to spring for candy. Passing out candy in the hallway was a key campaigning maneuver. VPs—of the USA or anywhere else—don't tend to have much on their to-do lists. This job, VP of the Liberty High School Senior Class, was also a cakewalk—or let's call it a candy walk.

Ring was running on a platform for change, but those changes weren't exactly revolutionary. One of the big ones was a guarantee to pick a cool prom theme. To give you an idea, the front-runners were Diana Ross's "Ain't No Mountain High Enough" and "I'll Be There" by the Jackson 5. These were crucial decisions, deserving of a conscientious leader.

Jeff and I plastered the school with posters, but we were pretty confident it wouldn't be necessary. Ring was a shoo-in.

However, he did have an opponent in the race. Against all odds, it was the captain of the cheerleaders, one Amy Kline. We had not spoken much since that day last fall at the bus stop. It wasn't really out of any hard feelings, although I definitely think she avoided me for a while after what happened. I didn't vilify her for it. The way I saw it, Billy was the real villain, if only in the high school sense.

I guess all of us who trudged through those murky swamps of teenagedom had at one time or another put on the villain's cape, mostly from the temporary madness that accompanied those years. At any rate, Billy had long since graduated and moved on to post–high school obscurity, complete with wearing his letter jacket every day to work down at the auto parts store, and leaving his graduation tassel hanging from his rearview mirror in perpetuity.

Amy was as much a victim of the whole teenage experience as the rest of us. She had turned out to be a pretty nice girl who had already thrown her hat in the ring before learning that Ring was also running. It had taken Ring some time to see the light—meaning it took us some time to badger him into seeing it.

Jeff told me he was sitting in seventh period English, three seats in front of Amy, when Principal Davenport announced the student government candidates for each class over the intercom. When Ring's name was called, the whole class erupted into cheering and applause. The whole class, that is, except Amy. Her face went as white as a sheet. I really felt sorry for her, but such was the political life, I figured.

The real deciding factor in the whole race was not the posters, the campaigning, or even the candy. It was the speech in front of the whole student body. Generally speaking, it was a moment for candidates to do one of two things: to speak in dead earnest, telling everyone about all the reasons they want to serve their constituency for the common good, or to grandstand like an idiot and get the room laughing.

Clearly Plan B—playing the idiot—was the wiser strategy. Jokers made good VPs; everybody knew that.

I was very familiar with this process. Not only had I been an office-holder in every year of high school up to that point but I was running for the big office: president of the student council. This meant I was campaigning for myself as well. But I found out pretty quickly that expending my political energy on Ring's behalf was the equivalent of pouring gasoline on the glowing coals of my own candidacy. It wasn't about going for "sympathy votes." I was campaigning for one of my best friends—and after all we'd been through, experiencing a moment with mutual benefits wasn't so bad.

Ms. Myers had taken over for Mrs. Gaines as the student council sponsor, and all candidates were instructed to meet in her room after school to get final details for the election. Ring and I strolled in late, as usual. I eventually got past my shame in using him as an ongoing excuse for tardiness. Again, mutual benefits.

"Nice of you to join us, gentlemen," Ms. Myers said with a little smile. I had taken her psychology class during junior year, and aced the final. Ring had been in the class with me. We studied together, mulling over superegos and lotuses of control and the like. Because of his fine motor skills being not so fine, handwritten assignments were a real challenge to his scholastic success, mainly because of the excessive time it took him to write.

Ms. Myers was one of the first teachers at Liberty High who could see that Ring was very intelligent—and that his writing issues were purely physical. She allowed me to sit next to him and write the answers for him as he said them out loud. We had to be on an honor system to do it, but we both had the feeling that since Ms. Myers was willing to help so much, we needed to avoid screwing that up. We wanted to be trustworthy. We wanted to make her proud.

I think she sensed this. And when Ring's psychology grade was almost as high as mine—he was able to score highly on oral tests—she "ran interference" for him with other teachers and showed them the best ways to work with him in the classroom.

It was a bit complicated, to say the least, because Ring was in mainstream classes, not special education ones. Thus there was a certain expectation that if he had been admitted to the class like everyone else, he should be able to participate in the class like everyone else. He was somewhere in the gray area between special education and special treatment—and neither would have been right.

Ms. Myers understood this, so she went to bat to help bridge the gap. Some teachers were pretty resistant to the idea, but she fought for Ring. She put it all on his shoulders, telling them that he did not need special treatment at all—he simply needed the ability to show exactly how able and intelligent he was, without being limited by the physical constraints of his cerebral palsy.

It took a few weeks and a lot of conversations, but she eventually won the day. The teacher for each of Ring's classes would ask for volunteers who would be willing to write answers for him as he dictated to them. This was the process only for worksheet and homework assignments. Ring still took his own notes, even if they were messy and he fell behind. But the teachers did allow other students to share their notes with him so he could complete whatever he had missed.

And the oral tests were always administered by the teachers or a teacher's aide.

Ms. Myers—a lot like my mom and dad—was the kind of adult who paid attention to life as it was, not life as the stiffer rules dictated. Many grown-ups just saw us when we had problems. Others just looked past us, or even through us. But some of them—the special ones—actually looked at us.

I always felt that Ms. Myers was watching us, from that first day she thought I had knocked Ring's books out of his hand. She didn't just pity Ring, as so many people did. She saw what he could be—that he was more than his disability. She never babied him. On the contrary, in the sense of pure academics she was one of the toughest teachers he ever had.

Simple answers were not sufficient for her. She made him dig deeper. Some teachers would let him skate by for one of two reasons. Either they were pitying him because so much energy was required to give even a simple answer, or they didn't have the patience to wait for him to spit it out.

Not Ms. Myers. She didn't care if it took all afternoon—and Ring knew this. Even he had been known to hide behind his special needs when he really wanted to be done with something, adding a little extra stutter here or a delay there. Spreading things out so the teacher would finally relent and everyone could be done and off to their next task.

But Ms. Myers somehow had a mental immunity against this particular trick. "Now, David, I know what you are doing. We're not leaving this room until you give me the definition of altruism. Come on, you know this."

And when she pushed him, it would turn out that he really did know it. She was firm with us, but throughout the course of that year she also became somewhat of an adult friend—something different from a friend your own age. The boundaries of respect and communication were still very much intact, but there were moments when she would laugh with us. I mean really laugh. And when you talked, you always knew she was listening. Not just hearing—keenly listening.

We could also tell that we were her favorites, which supposedly didn't exist in the adult sphere of reality. But everyone knew otherwise. Adults were not able to hide their true feelings, especially in moments of unrestrained laughter or in reactions of extreme irritability. When a teacher finally blew her top or laughed her head off, you could tell which kid was a trigger and which kid was a treasure.

At times, we were both—and she was the kind of person who liked it that way. To her, banter was an expression of affection. It was business as usual and when it came to us, business was very good.

Since this Tuesday meeting was after school, her comment about our tardiness was more sarcastic than serious. I replied in like kind. "Sorry, Ms. M! I had to wait for Ring to finish trying out for the track team—that hundred-yard dash was more like a hundred-yard doozy."

The students laughed at my joke, but Ms. Myers just shook her head. "Very funny, Mr. Wideman. Very funny." As the room was filled with student government candidates, it was a bit different than walking into a normal classroom, mainly because all the front row seats were occupied. Ring and I found seats in the back.

"I am so glad that each of you have decided to engage in our governmental process here at Liberty High. You live in a democracy, where it is very important that citizens learn at an early age what it means to carry the responsibility of a republican process." She also taught government, which was becoming more apparent as our eyes began to glaze over from her vocabulary. "But as much as I know you want to hear all about the joys of political science, we should probably talk about your speeches this Friday at the all-school assembly."

Ring's face turned pale. He turned to me as she kept talking. "Speeches?" he whispered, or attempted to whisper. "What speeches?"

"Dude, you knew that you had to make a speech. Everyone does, every year."

"I didn't know it was wequiwed!" His whisper was more of a rasp. Lesley Thompson turned around and shushed us. Typical.

"Ring, come on, man. You'll be fine. All you have to do is tell them who you are and what you want to do. It will be a piece of cake."

He was obviously not convinced. It was the first time in a long time I had seen him clam up like this. He had just been a different guy for so long. The last thing I had expected was a relapse to the "old" Ring.

Ms. Myers was finishing up her instructions. "So here is a sheet with the guidelines so that you young firebrand orators will not lose your minds and do something crazy on Friday. And remember, getting elected by laughter is not honorable."

Ring and I each took a sheet. His hands were shaking as he read it. I knew that the shaking was not just from his cerebral palsy. His nerves were bringing the tremors more than anything.

"I don't want to insult your intelligence by reading it to you," she continued, "but just for argument's sake, I think it would be wise to review a couple of items. Please note that you need to dress the part—girls in dresses and boys in ties. You should take this seriously. In life, when you take something seriously—whether it be a job interview or a college interview—you should always dress for success." A collective moan rose from the classroom. Remember, this was 1970.

"There will be no profanity or anything inappropriate said from the microphone. I am not shy. I will walk out across the auditorium platform, take the microphone from you, and remove you from contention in this race. Is that understood?" There was not much of an audible response. "Excuse me, aspiring politicians! Is that understood?"

"Yes, ma'am," we all replied, acknowledging that we understood and accepted her terms—not that we really did.

"And finally, you have exactly three minutes per speech. No more. Less is fine, but more is not. If you go over your three minutes, we will turn off your microphone."

She spoke a few more words of instruction, then the meeting was over. As always, Ring and I were the last ones to leave. Ms. Myers was straightening piles of papers and gathering her own things to leave. We walked out the door with her as she took out her keys to lock it behind us.

"I am very excited to hear your speeches this Friday." She smiled. "I know you're going to make me proud." We walked through the empty hallway toward the big blue doors at the end. There was a janitor sweeping up candy wrappers and campaign posters that were really just blank pieces of paper with colorful, handwritten words and designs on them.

"Yes, ma'am. It should be fun." I was trying to sound positive, as I had not yet had time to figure out what was going on with Ring—he was staring at the floor as we walked. He hadn't acknowledged that either of us had said anything at all.

Ms. Myers bit her upper lip as she studied us. She was always perceptive. "Mr. Ring? Is everything okay?"

He was stoic. "Ms. Myuhs, I can't do a speech. Yuh heuh how I tawk."

She didn't even break stride before she answered. "Yes, David, I hear how you talk. And there is nothing wrong with it. I've watched you in this school for a long time. You speak through your life, not just your mouth. Your actions talk every day."

"But—but I don' know what to sayee."

"Speak what's in your heart, David. What this world does not need is another person who sounds like everyone else. The world needs your unique voice."

He looked up at last and made eye contact with her. His blue eyes seemed to have layers, as if the color was only the lid of a kaleidoscope of other colors hidden somewhere beneath. He was definitely in a different world now.

He was no longer defined by the dark basement. But for the first time in a while, he was afraid. I guess I had missed it. I had so thoroughly taken for granted his metamorphosis that I had stopped watching for caterpillar behavior. I hadn't even considered the speech being a problem. To me, Ring wasn't some guy with a disability. He was just some guy.

But life was a little more complex than that. What he was being required to do was the epitome of everything he could not do physically. This was not a moment for school spirit. This was a moment of personal performance. No one would be able to speak for him when he stepped up to that microphone. No one would be able to fight for him against bus stop bullies or rival school ridiculers. He would have to stand and deliver on his own—and for the first time in his life, everyone was going to see the full scope of his limitations in real-time direct comparison to his peers.

Ms. Myers stopped walking, thus bringing us to a halt as well. "David, I will help you prepare your speech. Let's meet every day after school to practice, okay?"

"Okay." He mumbled it, but at least he said it. None of us, including him, were convinced.

21

That Friday

The rest of the week flew by pretty quickly. We were both busy with election stuff, barely finding time to talk about anything else. I know it wasn't fair, but I think I put Ring's impending speech in an "out of sight, out of mind" category. It was a compartment I just didn't have time—or perhaps the mental fortitude—to dwell upon.

I guess I was just hopeful. But I wasn't very helpful. Ms. Myers' offer of help had let me off the hook. Ring would come home with me for at least a couple of hours every day after school. Still, we didn't talk about it. We just made small talk. We coexisted. And we both knew we were doing it. I had dragged him into this, but now he was going to have to drag himself out. It wasn't intentional. It was just reality.

Friday morning found many of us guys sporting colorful neckties and oversized blue blazers, mostly borrowed from our fathers. There was a distinct olfactory current of after-shave drifting through the hallway—evidence that none of us really knew how much to apply. It was like we were using Afta or Old Spice to compensate for nervousness. But instead we were still nervous and everyone also had headaches.

The girls were a bit more with it. It was obvious that the females actually had experience dressing up—and by the looks of it, not by force. They actually enjoyed the very thing the guys loathed. Some had their hair pulled up, while others had it let down. They wore nice dresses and they proved that they knew just the right amount of perfume to use. They were good at this stuff.

I dated a few girls in high school, but mostly I never got serious with anyone. Days like this reminded me why. At least four times that day, various primped and painted beauties glided past me in the hallway or in class—the enchanting airborne wake of their shampoo and perfume leaving me as love-struck as Odysseus's men captivated by the song of the sirens. So many sirens! I knew I was too young to choose just one—yet.

The assembly was scheduled during second period, so there wasn't much time to waste. I spent most of first-period homeroom going over my speech—and trying not to think about Ring. I just hoped that Ms. Myers had prepared him. All I could do was hope.

A long semicircle of chairs had been placed out on the auditorium stage, which just crossed into the word *Blue-jays* painted at half court. The chairs were made of a blue composite material attached to polished aluminum tubing. I suppose every cafeteria in the nation had these same blue chairs at the time—and every one of them was a piece of junk that constantly chipped and was so heavy it scuffed up floors of any kind.

At the center of the seating arrangement was a small wooden podium with a long silver microphone emerging out the top. We were all allowed to leave homeroom a little early to head to the assembly and get ready. On my way to the gym, I stopped by Ring's homeroom so we could walk together.

He wore a pair of khaki pants with a white dress shirt my dad had bought for him. There was also a green tie, on loan from my dad, as well as brown loafers.

"Hey man! You look great. You ready for this?"

He was back in his Franciscan monk posture—and it appeared he had taken a vow of silence. Our walk to the gym was so solemn and foreboding that all we were missing was someone chanting behind us, "Dead man walking!"

Ms. Myers met us at the door to the gym. "Good morning, young men! You look absolutely excellent today. You both clean up so nicely!"

I thought she was right. I had one of my dad's blazers—complete with a tie swirling with very cool psychedelic colors. And I had actually put a little pomade in my hair, combing it to one side neatly. I was never one to brag, but I felt like a fresh hundred-dollar bill.

However, Ring's face immediately showed Ms. Myers that there were some things that could not be combed, ironed, or bathed away. He looked mortified, as if he might be sick. I knew she was alarmed, but that she would do what she could to keep him calm. She offered an expansive smile.

"You're ready, David. Just like we practiced."

"I'll twy." It was the first thing I had heard him say all day.

We were allowed to pick our seats in the semicircle. The speeches were not going to be made in any particular order. The administration really wanted to limit direct competition and negative back-and-forth among opposing candidates, even though the races were head-to-head. The speeches were supposed to be more than just simple popularity contests. The hope was that they would be solid exercises in developing public speaking skills, knowledge of the political process, and an overall sense of courage.

The only structure to the process was one's grade level. The speeches would begin with a random drawing from the freshmen candidates, in no particular order. Then sophomores. And so forth and so on.

I sat next to Ring. It was the best show of support I had left to lend him. Finally the floodgates were opened, bringing forth the deluge of the student body. I was shocked by the thundering sound of all those kids entering the gym. It was just normal conversation, conversation I was used to being a part of on a regular basis. But sitting up front and watching, I got a whole different perspective. For a moment, I realized I was hearing what teachers hear—then I caught myself and snapped back into a comfortable teenage state of mind.

They filed in from two different doors, staring at us as they found their seats. The school was small, but the gym was smaller. Students were packed in like sardines and seemed to be sitting on top of each other. A few waved or held up a thumb. A few held up other fingers in jest.

I looked across the circle of candidates and noticed that most of us were engaging with the people entering, laughing and smiling. Waving back. This was a campaigning moment—our friends could size us up side-by-side with the competition. I realized I thrived under such pressure, for whatever reason. So did most of the others, grinning and waving and showing off.

Then my eye fell on Ring. White as a ghost. Forehead beaded up with sweat. Hands probably clammy. He was taking this moment so seriously. Too seriously. And there was nothing I could do about it.

Principal Davenport stepped up to the podium and called the students to order. It took a few attempts, but eventually they calmed down—with the help of plenty of finger-pointing and authoritarian shushes from the faculty.

Once it was quiet, a few nameless, faceless voices would shout out from the crowd, "Go Wideman!" and "Do your thing, Ring!" Everyone laughed. And even Ring seemed to smile a bit. Maybe he was going to pull it off. Just maybe.

The freshmen speeches were pretty brutal, as was to be expected. They were either annoyingly overconfident, something we upperclassmen hated in freshmen (considering it was their job to be as awkward and scared as we had been in those days). Or they were too bubble-eyed, sweaty, and poorly spoken. So no matter what they did, I figured the freshmen were doomed. And that felt right.

Sophomores and juniors were much better. Andy Flankman came pretty close to breaking Ms. Myers' rules. He definitely played the stand-up comic, and several times he came right to the edge of cursing before retreating to safety. The result was riotous laughter from the crowd, who "heard" what he didn't say. It was pretty low-class by the Myers Manifesto, but such is politics, I suppose.

Then came the seniors. Poor Amy Kline was picked to go first. She did a solid job, speaking clearly and articulating with professionalism the intricacies of the needs of the senior class. The faces of the student body were neutral—neither negative nor accepting. And at one point, someone shouted out, "Bring the Ring!" Amy's face turned red, but she finished strong as a teacher pulled the heckler out of the crowd and escorted him to detention.

I went after Amy. It was a solid performance, if I do say so myself. Dad and I had worked on it for weeks, making sure I was inserting a good mix of both information and inspiration. And then, at the end, I threw in a healthy "Go Bluejays!" for good measure. The applause was heartening, and I was confident that things would go well in the election.

Things were going well, with one strange exception. Name after name was called, and speech after speech was given, but the call for Ring never came. Amy Kline. David Wideman. Jason Whitehead. Anna Worley. The names kept coming in random order, but never his. And the audience demand kept growing—they wanted to hear Ring.

Sure enough, he was the last speaker at the assembly. What were the odds? Even old stuffy Principal Davenport seemed to have a certain flare in the tone of his voice when he walked up to announce him. "And to close out today's student government election assembly program, running for vice president of the senior class. Last, but certainly not least, Mr. David Ring."

The gym erupted like it had so many times before when Ring had come to the center of the crowd's attention. I looked over at Amy—she was clapping too, almost as if she would rather him win this thing than herself. Maybe she felt it too: the sense of being a part of something greater than ourselves, such a rare feeling for our age.

I had been paying so much attention to the cheering crowd and the other candidates that I hadn't noticed Ring was still sitting beside me. He was staring at the podium, but I could tell he was not really looking there. He was somewhere else altogether—and it didn't seem to be a good place.

I nudged him with my elbow. "Ring, come on, man. You're up, dude."

Nothing. He just sat there.

Someone in the crowd decided to help him out a bit, and they started chanting his name. "Ring! Ring! Ring!" The chorus began slowly and quietly, but soon it grew in momentum. Someone added a clap to it. This was his moment to shine—his moment to show them what he had to say. Everyone was on his side. They were begging for him. But he just sat there in what seemed to be a state of paralysis.

I looked over at Ms. Myers. She seemed to be wincing as she bit her upper lip again. Her face said it all: this was painful to watch. The cheers continued until they erupted into applause. But once a fever pitch was reached, the crowd's jubilation had nowhere to go but down. And sure enough, the chant began to diminish, draining out of the room until it was gone, replaced by puzzlement. And whispers. A whole lot of whispers.

Then it happened. Suddenly, Ring stood up. As straight as I'd ever seen him. He looked like a two-by-four standing on its end. And the crowd literally went wild. He was still looking at the podium, but now he also seemed to be seeing it. Then he began to walk toward it—that unique walk of his. The students continued to cheer, but the whispers also continued. Everyone knew this was more painful than it should be for a student election. They had gotten so used to the big smile on his face, and what they saw now was more than nerves.

He finally stood behind the podium. He looked up at the crowd, then he looked over at Ms. Myers. The liveliness died down until the gym felt silent. Now Ring stood in front of a crowded room full of people. The spotlight was his. I prayed. Then I prayed some more.

Suddenly, he backed away from the podium and stood there a second. Then he turned to his left and began walking away from it as fast as he could. Painfully fast. I hustled to catch up with him, but as I went to put my hand on his shoulder, he swatted it away as he would a gnat. Then he glared at me—not the way he had a year ago. This was less anger and more pain. And I had no idea why I seemed to be a part of it.

I stopped trying to walk with him, stopped at the blue free-throw line where I had taken so many shots during PE these past four years. Ring quickly exited out the huge metal doors, hitting the stainless steel bar as hard as he could to open it. When it closed behind him, the sound reverberated throughout the room like we were in an echoing canyon.

I turned back around and realized I was now the only person standing in the gym. Everyone else was sitting, turning in my direction, staring. My face went red—I could feel it in my cheeks and my ears. The whispers were now deafening and I quickly returned to my seat, not knowing what else to do. I looked over and locked eyes with Ms. Myers—her face was now as white as Ring's had been.

This was a disaster. I began telling myself that I had inadvertently caused the whole thing. I had pushed him to do this—the one thing he simply could not do and would never be able to do: speak in public. He left me standing on that floor by myself so I would feel just a bit of what he had felt. Really just a microcosm. His pain was a nest of wasps and mine was but a little anthill.

Principal Davenport put away the unraveled look on his face and tried to reclaim the moment at the microphone.

"Okay, students, remember that voting is a part of your constitutional rights, so everyone take it seriously. You will be voting in your third-period class and we will announce the winners at the end of the day. You are dismissed to your third-period class."

I couldn't find Ring the rest of the day. He didn't show up at our lunch table. He didn't show up to our English class. He even missed football practice, which made Coach H pretty unhappy. When I finally got home that evening, he wasn't there either. I told Dad all about what had happened at the assembly. We waited up for hours, but Ring never came by. I guess since it wasn't really his home, he was allowed to not come by. But I felt his absence painfully.

22

Later That Morning

Ring moved as fast as his two legs would allow. He cursed those legs, which were as much against him as everything else in the world was, and he looked out at the traffic.

There weren't many cars running up and down Nashua Road during this morning hour. Mainly a few service and delivery trucks here and there, and a few old ladies heading to get groceries.

He had walked this way before, back when he was almost run over by that tractor trailer. But today he was not walking with any intention of trying something like that again. He was walking without any intentions at all. He just needed to get *away*.

The nausea had at least subsided. But he couldn't drive the picture from his mind. All those eyes. All those faces. All those ears perked up and ready to hear his pathetic attempt at speaking. Heck, his attempts at just talking were pretty pathetic. He pondered the differences between speaking and talking. To him there was a vast difference, and he was a dismal failure at both.

He came to the elementary school. There were a few classes of first or second graders on the playground. They were running and screaming with pure joy. These kids were lost in their own Neverlands and Sherwood Forests and Lands of Oz. They ran about unfettered by anything, especially reality. He watched the marvel of their movement, their grace, their sheer, rosy-cheeked health.

Reality was all Ring had: cold, uncaring reality. He'd never live a single day with those children's abilities. It all might as well be fantasy from *Peter Pan* as far as he was concerned. Life for him was no storybook. It was a tragedy. He was crippled, and he had never felt so deeply so. That morning's disastrous speech revived something in him that he'd thought he'd buried forever: hopelessness. He had watched the other students make their jokes and use their voices, and he realized now what he'd felt as he watched these kids: he could never really fit in.

Sure, that night at the Widemans' church had changed things. He had learned that God could make something out of nothing. He'd been reading the book of Genesis a lot since then. It showed how God did that over and over. Worlds sprang forth from the simple snap of his fingers. Land emerged out of the sea. Birds and fish and animals and plants—they began flying and creeping and crawling just because he told them to.

But mostly, Ring was struck by Adam's birthday. God drew in the dust, making the outline of a man. This seemed to be different from all the rest of creation. When it came to

Adam, God began with something instead of nothing. And he began with something seemingly worthless and without hope. Dust.

Ring wondered if God had stood over that rudimentary dust sketch and sighed. It couldn't have looked like much. A small breeze blew through Eden, blurring the lines of one of the arms. Ring imagined God laughing, then taking his finger and redrawing that part.

Then he breathed.

Oh, what a breath that must have been! Ring had played a lot in the dirt when he was younger—it was the main playground for poor kids in Arkansas. For that matter, it was the main playground for any kids in Arkansas. Since no other kids had wanted to play with him, he had become a self-entertainer. A dirt artist. He had drawn trucks and airplanes and a hundred other things in the dirt, imagining flying over Berlin in a dogfight or cruising the highways or sailing the sea.

But none of these things ever lived outside of his imagination. Ring's creations simply went away, blown about by the wind or dissipated by a hard rain. God's dirt drawings had actually become something. Someone, even.

Ring didn't just feel like nothing. He felt like something hopeless. Something with no value. Something worse than nothing. He was something made of dust. But for a period of time, he had thought God was breathing into him. His usefulness and his role on the football team. His newfound family, the Widemans. His three friends. His acceptance by his church family. His acceptance at school—heck, some might even call it popularity.

There had even been the courage to stand up to Debbie in the dark. All these things had felt like new life for him, life rising from the dust. As if he was no longer something made from hopelessness.

But this morning had come. This speech. This failure. That moment dragged him back down to earth—back into dust and dirt and nothingness. It made him feel as if all the transformation had been nothing more than a mirage.

He suddenly felt that God had drawn an outline of David Ring in the dirt—and then just left him that way. Dusty. Disabled. Debilitated. He was still imprisoned in his own body. Still shackled to his speech impediment.

No one in that gym had laughed at him. That might have made it easier. He could have vilified them and played the victim, retreating into himself. But instead he'd felt their pity. They didn't admire him—they just felt sorry for him. Who needed that?

Even so, they wanted him to succeed, even to lead—he couldn't deny that. But he was not able. He had let them all down.

This time he wasn't walking to try to end it all on an interstate. This time he was merely walking to be away from them—because he couldn't get away from himself. He knew there was no such thing as running away, literally or metaphorically. He was stuck in himself, but he didn't have to let all of them be stuck with him too.

He wasn't going to end it all, but he had no idea where to turn or what to do. He had too much to live for now—and that in itself was a new source of pain he had never anticipated.

He was walking through the parking lot of the Gulf station near the interstate exit when a turquoise Volkswagen Beetle pulled into the entrance near him. The paint was chipping in places above the driver's side window, which was rolled down. It rumbled at idle with that signature high-pitched engine sound that only VW Bugs had as it coasted up beside him, and he figured it was just another customer. Then a familiar voice called out from the open window.

"Mr. Ring! Where ya headed, traveler?"

He turned in shock to see Ms. Myers.

Her hair was pulled back in a ponytail. It was a rare moment to see a teacher outside of school, but it was even rarer to see one seem like an ordinary, everyday human being. She had a carefree look on her face, as if she were on her way to a picnic.

Ring was speechless—for the second time that day. He didn't want to be disrespectful, so he stopped walking.

"It wasn't that bad, you know," she said. "In fact, I found it quite refreshing. I have heard many speeches over the years that would have been much better if they had taken your approach."

"Yeah wight," Ring replied. "I was an idiot."

"I prefer to just call it the strong, silent type," she replied with a reassuring smile.

He did his best to reciprocate with a smile, but he couldn't seem to find one.

"You gonna walk to St. Louis, champ?"

He shrugged his shoulders. "I jus' needed to geh away. Am I in twoubuh?"

It was an honest question. As a matter of fact, maybe they both were in trouble; she had left school without permission too. All in all, this was new terrain—the surface of Mars or some alternate galaxy.

"Nah, I don't think we should get you in trouble today." She looked past him to the truck stop on the other side of the highway. "I hear they have sandwiches over there that aren't half bad. They aren't really half good either. But you know what they say, a sandwich is either half good or half bad—or was it that a glass is half empty or half full? I've never really been that good at aphorisms."

Ring actually laughed this time, but mainly at her tone of playfulness—he definitely had no idea what an aphorism was. "Okay. Wet's geh a sawwich."

She reached over and opened the passenger side door, and he made his way around the car to get in.

"Sorry," she said, "the door won't open from the outside. I need to get it fixed."

She moved a pile of books from the front seat to the back. *An Introduction to Psychology. The Common Sense Book of Baby and Child Care*. And a paperback novel lying on top of the stack featured a scantily clad man embracing an equally scantily clad woman—both seemed as if their flowing white clothes might randomly fall off of them at any moment.

"My car is such a mess. Sorry."

All of this suggested a Ms. Myers he had no idea even existed. He had always felt uncomfortable around women, but there was something about Ms. Myers. Something that made him feel safer. He shut the door and they made the short trek across the street. They sat down in a small booth—the seats were smooth and far from being padded. But still, he felt comfortable. She ordered for both of them.

"David, I know today was tough. You want to talk about it?"

"What's theh to tawk 'bout? I faiwed."

"You didn't fail. There's always another chapter after the last one. Always a chance for something to grow into something else."

"How can I eveh be something ewse? Wook at meh!" He didn't realize he had said it so loudly. He didn't want to be angry with her. It just came out on its own. "Sowwy."

"It's okay, David. I wish I could tell you that I know how you feel, but honestly, I don't. I don't blame you for being angry."

He listened to her intently, feeling a little better about what she had said. She continued, "But at the same time, what you are dealing with doesn't appear to be changing anytime soon. You can't let it be your constant reason for leaving every time things get tough."

His eyes got wider. "But I can't tawk wight. I can't wawk wight. There aw some things I just can't do."

"I disagree. You might talk differently, but that doesn't mean it's not right. You're letting what you think people think about you dictate what you think is right. And that's no way to live—not for someone like you."

"What do yuh mean, someone wike me? What do yuh know 'bout me?" Ring was not trying to be disrespectful. He was just not in the mood to be patronized.

"You know, that's a great question, David. I really don't know enough about you. Will you tell me more?"

Just then, the waitress brought them their drinks, a water and a Dr. Pepper. Ring sat silent for several moments, drawing small circles in the condensation on the side of his hard plastic cup.

"Well?"

Another few moments passed. He finally decided to grant her request. Why not?

For the next four hours, Ring told Ms. Myers everything from his story—everything, that is, except what Debbie had done. He couldn't tell that to anybody, regardless of his threats to Debbie that he would. He did tell her about his mom and dad. His sick brothers and the nearly twenty minutes he was dead as a baby.

He told her about Oscar's cotton gin accident. The divorce. Leron's cancer. The bullies. He told her everything—all the way down to the most difficult parts of his average day. The simple things like tying his shoes or writing his name.

At some point their sandwiches came to the table. Pimento cheese on one, ham and cheese on the other. As always, he didn't touch his. She was so engrossed in his story that she didn't touch hers either. By the looks of the food and the looks of the flies buzzing around it, they weren't very tasty anyway.

Ring spoke more that day than he ever had before, the story taking on a clarity new even to him. It was as if his mouth were a filter and all that was needed was for the story to pass through it—and then it came out clean. And he could see it in a brand-new way. For the first time he realized the power of opening the closet and letting the light shine on what was inside. Ms. Myers cried so much that the napkin dispenser on their table ran empty.

When he had finished she just sat there, dumbfounded and undone. "David, that was unbelievable. Do you have any idea how powerful your story is?"

He shrugged, searching for the right kind of reply to such a statement. "Maybe yuh could tew some of yo' students 'bout it in the fuchuh—maybe it wiw hewp someone."

"No, David! It is powerful because you are the one speaking it!" She looked him directly in the eyes, as if this conversation might change the trajectory of his life. "The very thing you are most worried about is the very thing you must use. David, I just sat here for hours and listened to you speak.

Others will do the same. I promise, others will listen and your story will affect them in ways you can never imagine."

"Me?" It was the first time he had ever thought about anything so crazy.

She continued. "Your greatest limitation is also your greatest asset. You just have to be brave enough to try."

"Buh the ewection is ovuh," he replied.

She sighed dismissively. "This is bigger than some student council election, David! This is bigger than all of us." She paused and looked out the window. It was nearly dusk. "We need to come up with some place for you to tell your story." She mumbled things as if to herself. Ideas. "You could talk to my classes. No—that's not big enough. More people need to hear this!"

"Mo' peopow?" Ring could feel a significant stirring in the pit of his stomach as she continued to craft her elaborate plan.

"It would take some work, but we need to plan an all-school assembly. It would be voluntary, obviously. After school, maybe. But we would invite everyone to come hear your story."

The churning in Ring's stomach continued to strengthen against the outlandish idea—but something else inside of him seemed to be opening up, to consider the possibility. Just consider it. That wasn't the same as accepting it. And he realized that was pretty crazy too, considering that only a few hours earlier he had choked in front of the whole school on a three-minute election speech. Life was upside down right now.

Ms. Myers paid the check for their uneaten sandwiches and the two of them walked out to the parking lot. "Mr. Ring, where am I taking you?"

"Nowheh, Ms. Myuhs. Bu' thank you."

"No, David. I insist. I'm not leaving you out here by yourself."

"Ms. Myuhs, this won' be the fust time I've been alone. Buh honessly, I jus' wan' to take a wahk and think. Thank yuh so much, buh I'll be fine." Part of him didn't want her to see where he lived—and more importantly, to run into who he was living with. But he was also being truthful; he needed some time to contemplate.

She shook her head and smiled. "All right, I can't make you accept a ride in my Beetle limousine. You be careful and I'll see you at school on Monday." Then she reached over and hugged him, something that would normally send any student running for cover. But it felt right—he knew he could trust her.

He didn't walk straight home. He took the long way. He stopped at the old sawmill and sat down on one of the loading docks near the river, letting his feet dangle as the moon rose to shine on the surface of the gently rolling water. He took a deep breath and lowered his head.

There he had a moment with God—a moment different from any other one he had ever experienced. Fear seemed to roll away with the current. Courage rose up within him in its place. He felt clean. Empowered. Mobilized to do something his heart had never even dreamed of.

That was the thing. That was how he knew it was real. The dream that was now taking its first breaths within him was not just a new thought. It was a new compartment of thought in his mind. A new area of his brain growing into existence before his very eyes—or rather behind his eyes. It was as outrageous to him as Moses's moment at the burning bush. No, even more so.

Yet it was undeniable.

He stayed there for hours, but it only seemed like a few minutes. And they were some of the most important hours of his life. When he left, his legs still limped. But there was no doubt he was walking straighter than he ever had before—than he had ever thought possible.

He needed to talk, to share the spark with someone, but there was no one at his own house who could be trusted. So he headed to the Widemans. By the time he made it there, everyone was already fast asleep. He remembered that Brother Don kept an old multicolored quilt in the back of his car parked in the driveway—and he never locked his car. It was still there from a summer outing when the whole family had taken a picnic together down at the Liberty City Park across from the church; he did not clean out his car very often.

Ring didn't want to wake the family, so he took the quilt and lay down on the old porch swing. It was rarely used, and the chains were beginning to rust, creaking as he lay down across the faded wood slats. It was such a warm night that he balled up the quilt and used it as a pillow. It was the most uncomfortable bed he had ever slept in, yet he never slept better than he did on that mild September night.

23

Saturday Morning

I was beyond groggy the morning after Ring fled from the assembly. It had taken me hours to get to sleep, and when I did at last, even my slumber seemed miserable.

I was awakened to the faint light of an early dawn and the unmistakable sound of mockingbirds. Just what I needed—their raucous "mocking" forcing me to wake up. As I stumbled down the stairs to breakfast, I wasn't in the best of moods. At least I didn't fracture any limbs in my semi-controlled descent.

I opened the refrigerator and proceeded to gulp down orange juice straight from the container. I knew Mom would kill me, but I was up early and it was that kind of morning. I began to rummage through the cabinets, looking for cereal, when I heard the sound of voices coming from the front porch.

I glanced out the little kitchen window over the sink. Then I looked again. Then I almost dumped the entire box of Cheerios onto the floor. There was my dad, sitting with Ring on our front porch. Ring was on the porch swing, and Dad was sitting in one of the kitchen chairs facing him.

Ring was slightly rocking back and forth on the swing with the exact force of something naturally swaying in the wind—on a day with little to no wind. He had an old quilt balled up in his lap. I processed what I was seeing and realized that Ring had slept on the porch swing last night.

Suddenly there were many things I needed to do. I needed to run out there and check on my friend. I needed to apologize for pushing him into running in the election and not thinking through how he might feel about giving a speech. I needed to make things right between us.

I needed to, but I couldn't. Not now, because I could tell Dad and my friend were having a serious conversation. Meaning there was no way I was not going to eavesdrop, even though it was none of my business. As I peeked through the window, I heard Dad's voice.

"David, it's a worthy thing you want to do. It really is, but—"

"Buh what? Yuh do et, Bwutha Don."

"I know I do. Listen, there's nothing wrong with you just being you. And there's nothing wrong with you just doing the things God has made you to do, just as you are."

Ring seemed pretty agitated, something I had never seen in him around my father. He had always looked up to him, out of admiration and respect. He responded to the compassion my dad had shown for him and to the way he had made himself available for Ring. I realized that Dad was the closest thing Ring had to a father of his own these days.

So it was strange to sense his frustration. He was trying to hide it, but the swing began making more and more creaks as he fidgeted and rocked faster.

"Yuh don' think I can do et, do yuh?" There was such pain in his voice.

"Ring, there are a lot of people out there who will fill your head with all kinds of thoughts. They will try to convince you that you have to do certain things in order to be great. All I am telling you is that you are already great just the way you are. Period."

Dad put his elbows on his knees and leaned in closer. "And you don't need to prove yourself to me, to your peers, or especially to God. You don't have to stand up and try to speak to the whole school—it just doesn't seem to me like something you were made to do. There is no shame in that. Please don't misunderstand me—we love you as if you're our own son. You know that. And I would tell my son the same thing."

I didn't quite know what they were talking about, other than the shocking indication that Ring wanted to speak to the whole school. I couldn't imagine how that could happen. The election was over. And I was with Dad on this one; why would Ring want to keep humiliating himself for no good reason? He was loved and valued—and that was enough. I wondered why it wasn't enough for him too.

Ring still didn't seem convinced. He seemed to be struggling internally through the course of this conversation. I could see it in his face and hear it in his pained words. For a minute, he just sat there swinging, looking at the patchwork on the old quilt and contemplating what to say. Finally, he stopped swinging and looked Dad directly in the eyes.

"Yuh ah wike a fathuh to meh. Yuh took meh into yo' home. I can nevuh wepay yuh. But las' night, God spoke to meh. He wans meh to tew peopow my stowy. He wans me to tew them 'bout him an' what he did in my whife. I have to do this. I need to do this."

His confidence was almost palpable—and over the very thing in his life that seemed impossible. I felt a cold chill, hearing the boldness of his statement.

But Dad didn't seem to share my sentiments.

"David, I'm not trying to squash any of your dreams. And I'm so glad you are hearing from God in your life. But God also gave you our family to protect you—that's what good parents and friends do for the people they love. I'm trying to protect you here, son. I think it is a bad idea, but only because I don't want to see you get hurt."

Then he paused and looked out across the street somewhere, but I was pretty sure he was not looking at something any of us could actually see. "Ministry is not a safe place, David. People don't know what it's like. But I do. We do. People need servants and shepherds and teachers, but they will also turn on you. They will reject you. And they will leave you in a heartbeat if you don't fully satisfy their every whim."

He looked Ring in the eye. "I love them anyway. I love them with every fiber of who I am. But I wouldn't be a very good friend—" With these words, a tear fell from his eye, and he paused to clear his throat. "I wouldn't be a good father if I didn't at least tell you the truth about how it works out there."

I was standing near the window, leaning against the wall, but I needed to shift my weight. When I did, I brushed our family portrait—an old black-and-white one from when I was much younger, mounted in a simple black metal frame.

It fell off the wall and hit the floor with a solid clunk. Against all odds, it didn't break the glass, but it did blow my cover.

"David? We hear you in there, son. Come on out."

Sheepishly I made my way out onto the porch.

"Hey. I was making some breakfast and, well . . ." I trailed off, not knowing what else to say.

Ring looked at me, "Dayvid, thanks fo' yestuhday. I'm sowwy I wan off aftewuds."

I was taken aback. "Come on, man. I should be the one apologizing to you! I should have thought about the speech. I should have used my head."

"No! What yuh did for meh was exacwy what I neededh, even if et didn't work out."

I raised an eyebrow. "What do you mean, didn't work out? No one's told you, have they?"

"Towd meh what?"

"Ring, they counted the votes. You won."

24

October 1970

The only person in this world more stubborn than Ms. Myers was David Ring. If the two of them got their heads together, nothing was going to stop their plan from happening.

That's why things moved at lightning speed. I wouldn't have thought of that plan in a million years, but it only took the two of them three weeks.

Maybe, as a psychology teacher, Ms. Myers wanted to do a social experiment. Who knows? The only thing I'm sure of is that she really believed in Ring and his story. She passionately bought into it, in that way that someone can't fake. Kind of like the way I felt about the Kansas City Chiefs, even though they had disappointed me so many times.

But this was no game. This was real life. And it seemed there was nothing Ring could do in this world to disappoint her.

I didn't hear many people around school discussing Ring and the assembly incident. I think most of them felt pretty sorry for him. So when I saw the yellow poster taped to a locker, I didn't know what to think except that Ring had apparently gone totally crazy or something. In all caps, it read:

COME SEE THE BOY BORN DEAD!

Below this were the details. There would be a voluntary assembly the next Thursday after school in the gym—Ring was returning to the scene of the crime, three weeks later. He was going to tell his life story.

As I walked to British Lit, the yellow leaflets seemed to be multiplying, taking over the hallway. And the speech incident that had been swept under the rug was now at the forefront of everyone's conversation. People knew he and I were good friends, and many of them asked me what this was all about. I felt pretty foolish because I really had no idea myself. As a matter of fact, I was worried about my friend.

So I stopped by Ms. Myers' class after school. She was washing her chalkboard with a sponge, something I always found oddly soothing to watch—like the exact opposite of scratching a dry chalkboard. The water just washed it all clean and made it so shiny.

"Ms. Myers," I said, "do you mind if I ask you a question?"

"I'm pretty sure you just did." She smiled at me with her unique smile that always followed a moment of banter. And she kept washing the board.

"Yes, ma'am, I suppose I just did."

"Okay, what is your real question?"

"What is this assembly thing with Ring all about? I'm just . . ." I paused because I wasn't sure what was going to come out of my mouth next. "I just don't want him to be embarrassed again for no reason. You know?"

She looked at me and stopped her work, placing the sponge in the small bucket of murky water on her desk. "You know, I think the problem is that you used the words 'no reason.' I think there is plenty of reason for Mr. Ring to do this if it's what he wants."

I did not expect that response from her. "I don't mean it like that. You know me. You know that I want the best for him, that's all."

"I know that, Mr. Wideman. And I appreciate it. I just think that his best is something yet to come—and it is something that is going to shock even you. And quite possibly the rest of the world too." Her air of activism and raw assurance was so appealing—that was why we all liked her so much.

She continued, "You're not the only one who is concerned. I've had quite a few teachers come to tell me they're opposed to this. I even had to have a meeting with Principal Davenport over it. I'll tell you what I told them: this is important for David Ring, as important as any basketball game, football game, election, or event that any other student in this school will ever have in their scholastic careers. This is his moment to shine and to show the world that he has something completely unique and special to say. He can't make it on the baseball field. He can't make it in Vietnam. He can barely make it on a piece of paper. Let's let him make it here. Let's let him make it right now, because right now he has something great to say."

She was so inspirational, and always had been. Even in her classes, when she spoke there was something that came alive inside of us that made us want to take up arms and storm the French Bastille—even if it started a revolution. No, especially if it started a revolution. She pulled the sponge out of the bucket and began wringing it out for another scrub. "And besides, it's completely voluntary, so there's no issue."

Despite my inner revolutionist, I still had my doubts. "Yeah, but what if no one comes? Won't that become the bigger issue?"

She looked at me intently. "Look, David, I've watched you with him over the past two years. I get it. I really do. And what you've done for him is more than admirable; it's amazing. Just look at who he has become! And we know that in most high schools, this is not who he would be. Here he's had a protector. He's had a friend. He's had you and your family."

I could feel tears welling up against my every effort to restrain them. She continued, "Look, I've not been the most religious person in the world. I've not even been in the top ten, for that matter."

I managed to chuckle a bit, which gave me temporary relief from the overwhelming emotions I was trying to corral.

"But watching you and Mr. Ring and then hearing the incredible story that he has lived—well . . ." She shook her head, and this time I could see that there were restrained tears in her eyes too. "I don't know, David. I guess for the first time in my life, I see something in someone else that makes me want to believe in something bigger than myself. I know that may not mean much to a preacher's kid, but for someone like me, it's a pretty big start."

This was definitely uncharted territory for me. I had some experience with adults sharing their feelings, as I had seen countless people do so with my dad. But now, as I stood on the precipice of a new season of adulthood in my own life, a teacher—the pinnacle position of authority in my life—was cracking the door to let me see just a bit of what was going on in her own soul.

But beyond that, I was struck by the knowledge of whose slow-moving foot was stuck in that crack, holding the door open—Ring's. Up to this point, I had agreed with my father on everything in life. Everything important, at least. I had no reason not to. And to some extent, I still agreed with him on this point.

I knew that what Dad had said on the porch was right. Ring was different. He would be treated with contempt in a way none of us could ever know. Because he had lost more, he somehow had more to lose. It was an unfair reality I had lived with only subconsciously up until now.

But Dad had been more than fully aware of it from the first moment Loretta asked for his help at church. He knew the painful truth about a cruel world—a truth I would come to grips with myself in the years to come. Ring would experience pity in a way that devalued his humanity. He would experience ridicule in a way that would rob him of equality. And he would experience loneliness in a way that would isolate him utterly.

Dad had known this all along, which made his willingness to bring him into our home that much nobler. He knew what he was getting into with Ring; I was just beginning to understand the scope of it. It was more than just a few years of friendship or a few fights against bullies. It was more than bringing him into our social circles or buying him a burger down at Kuku.

His life was his—for life.

But this very epiphany I was having about Dad was also the one bringing me to a gradual disagreement with him. Disagreement may have been too strong a term. Perhaps it was more actually the fact that I was torn over it. I understood Dad's fatherly instincts to protect Ring at all costs—but I was also young and idealistic. Ring had made me believe in miracles. I wanted to have faith that the miracle had no limits.

I loved and trusted my dad. I simply needed to experience this moment for myself. To dream for Ring for myself. And I was seeing what that dream could truly be through the eyes of my psychology teacher. His story of tragedy and redemption had already planted seeds of transformation in her life. And I couldn't help but feel that I was in the middle of what I had been taught about Jesus all my life—taught by Dad.

He was right about things. He just didn't know how far his "rightness" extended.

The waves of this new revelation washed over me, the undertow pulling me farther out into the sea of pure hope and faith. When Ms. Myers spoke again, I was almost startled.

"What happened at the election speech was not what I think will happen here. Ring didn't leave because of his voice or his disability. He left because he really didn't have anything to say. 'Vote for me' was not his real life message. I have to tell you that I have heard what this young man does have to say—and when it's time for him to deliver it, I am fully confident that he will and that people will listen. We can talk all day long about his special needs, but the truth is, the students in this school also have a lot of needs—and 'special' ones at that. It's not just Ring's needs we should be thinking about right now—it's theirs too. They need to hear this. They need to hear David Ring."

Her words resonated with me. I was beginning to buy in, but she wasn't done. She put her hand on my shoulder and said, "We all want to protect Ring, David. But that's not what he wants right now. And for one of the first times in my life, I want what he wants. I want to believe."

My answer came more quickly than I thought it would. The words erupted out of me because I so badly wanted them to. "I do too." I smiled at her and shook my head affirmatively a few times. "I do too."

I picked up my bag to leave as Ring walked into the classroom. He was carrying a stack of flyers for the upcoming assembly. When he saw me, his face dropped. "Hey, Dayvid. What aw yuh doin' heuh?"

"Actually, I was just talking to Ms. Myers about the assembly."

"Yeah, I know wha' yuh think 'bout et. Yo' daddy aweady towd meh evewything."

He was hurt over the conversation with my father—and that hurt me.

"Ring, Dad doesn't mean anything by it. He's trying to protect you, that's all."

"I know he is, buh I don't need mo pwotection. I need fwiends who will hewp meh do wha' God wants meh to do."

"And what is that, exactly?"

Ms. Myers seemed mesmerized by the conversation we were having, as if she knew she had a front row seat to a dialogue that would change the course of our very lives. Everyone knows that these moments happen somewhere in the teen years—when dies are cast and courses are set that change the destination of one's future. But I could tell by her face that these moments, everyday as they must be, were things teachers rarely got to witness firsthand. Teachers get stuck with the eye-rolls and responsibility speeches and essays to grade. But now she was seeing something real.

Ring didn't look down or away. He had a distinct confidence in his voice. "Yuh know wha' I am goin' to do? I am goin' to be a twavwing pweacha—I'm goin' to tew people who aw huwting wike me 'bout the hope I found in God and the fwiendship of his peopow. I'm goin' to twavel the wouhd!"

His words were absolutely outrageous. Even asinine. This boy could barely make his way down the hallway and his words were almost incomprehensible to those who didn't know him well.

But that ember of hope suddenly glowed inside me with renewed heat. I began to walk in faith, discarding the crutches of logic and conventional wisdom. Ring's eyes were a deep and constant blue, and they beckoned me to join him in this craziness.

I reached out my hand toward him. "If you need a friend with you in this dream, then you got one. Let's do this."

He stared at my hand for a moment and then smiled widely. He reached out and shook my hand, but then pulled me close for a hug. A brotherly one, with lots of awkward back patting and nervous laughter. When we finished, Ms. Myers had tears streaming down her face.

I sat down in one of the desks and reached in my bag to pull out a notebook and pencil. "Okay, if we're going to do something crazy, where do we start?"

The days passed quickly as we pulled every social string we had in the school. Jeff came on board in no time. We knew that the event would not disappoint in terms of attendance. But the delivery was another matter altogether. I tried to keep my emotions in check, refusing to be overprotective of Ring. Like he said, this was his dream. His calling. His moment.

I felt terrified, but I also felt alive. And I loved that I was feeling something for his sake, not just for myself. I truly felt that I had something to lose because he did. But I also felt that I had something to gain because he did. No matter what I felt with each fleeting moment of the process, I was embedded in it and this event was happening.

On the Monday of the week of the event, I came home from school to find Dad sitting in the porch swing, something he never did. But it was as if Ring's sleeping there had made it a site of some significance. Positional memory, I suppose. At any rate, he looked contemplative. He was thumbing through a small book, reading, but mainly gazing out at the yard.

"Dad, you okay?"

"You know I always want the best for you kids, right?"

It was a strange question—and something I had never questioned.

"Of course. Why would you even ask such a thing?"

"Ring."

I leaned up against the wall. "Ring is fine, Dad. He's a little upset that you don't seem to want him to do this speaking thing, but don't worry—he knows that you want the best for him. We all do."

"When you were a little boy—maybe two or three—I used to lie down with you every night as you fell asleep. We would read a bedtime book and you would usually want me to wrestle, even though your mother didn't like it because it would get you all riled up again before bed. So we'd 'quiet wrestle,' but you could never keep yourself from laughing. She always knew what we were doing—and she would give me that look."

He paused in thought for a moment, remembering, then looked at me. "But when the lights went out, your mom would come in and sing a few songs, and then we'd pray with you. I always prayed that you would sleep all night and have fun dreams. That you would not be afraid of anything. And that your path would be clearly set before your feet. A path that would lead you to a good wife. A fulfilling career. A long life."

He paused to bite the edge of his fingernail. "You may not remember all of that, son, but those things are in you. They are planted deep in a place you cannot see. But they are growing. Affecting you. And they always will."

He placed a hand on my shoulder. "You see, son, I didn't get to do that with Ring. I didn't get to protect him or speak those positive things into his life when he was small. So that's what I'm trying to do now. To keep him safe, because no one has ever done that for him. I don't want him to be afraid, but I also don't want him to jump off a cliff without a parachute. Maybe I'm the parachute?"

I noticed the last part was a question, not a statement. He was agonizing over that talk with Ring.

I said, "Dad, Ring is not a baby. He's a man. And he knows you are a good man."

He didn't say anything in reply. I kind of understood why, though it seemed like it should have insulted me. The little boy with whom he snuggled every night was now giving counsel to the counselor.

"Dad, are you going to come on Friday to hear him?"

He sat looking at the rusty chain of the swing, touching it lightly and then blowing the flecks from his hand, and finally wiping his hand on his trousers. He did this nervously for a long while before answering.

"I can't. I just can't."

I shook my head just a bit, biting my bottom lip to keep myself from crossing the line into territories of conversation I knew were out of my jurisdiction; he had the right to his own strong opinions.

25

That Friday

It was here: Friday afternoon. D-Day. When the final bell rang, the hallways filled with students as usual. But on this day, the weekend would be an hour late getting started. Students filed like cattle from their lockers toward the gym.

It had only been a matter of weeks since they had come to the same place to hear speeches. But that half-circle of chairs had been removed. There was only a podium and a microphone—and a room full of antsy curiosity.

I sat in the front row with Ring as the bleachers filled up behind us. He had a few notes in his hands that Ms. Myers had helped him compile. He was reading them to himself, his lips slightly, silently moving. I noticed that the pages were shaking feverishly, as if a stout breeze were blowing through his fingers.

"You okay, Ring? Anything else I can do?"

I knew this was a difficult place for him. He was obviously very nervous, but he had brought all of this upon himself, insisting that this event happen against the counsel of my father and, in the beginning, myself. He didn't look up at me, but instead just said, "This is my momen'."

And it was. Ready or not, it was here. The gym suddenly seemed much bigger than it usually was, as if it had expanded with the heat of the moment. The usual outbursts of teenage energy, layers of loud laughter and conversation, echoed from the rafters to the hardwood floor.

Ms. Myers walked to the podium and tapped the microphone, which made a loud squeal, lifting the students' collective posture like a puppeteer's strings. Then a silence set in—a silence that no normal school assembly could ever produce, not in a hundred years of detention threats or cold stares from teachers. This was because for the first time in their lives, they had come voluntarily to listen to someone speak to them.

Among the attentive were faculty and staff, from Principal Davenport to the receptionist Mrs. Egden. Even the school janitor had propped himself up against the blue mat on the wall behind the basketball hoop. Everyone who in any way made up Liberty High School was there.

"Good afternoon, students. What a great turnout today to listen to a story that I know will influence your life." She paused and looked down as if she had notes, even though she had none. "I know because it has influenced mine." She glanced over at the two of us and smiled warmly.

"You've seen the flyers in the hallway advertising that you should 'Come see the boy born dead.' I know this may sound a little insensitive to some of you, but trust me, no description could be more accurate. The young man you are about to listen to is someone you love, but I doubt he is someone you fully know. Today, he would like to give you the opportunity to change that. So without any more delay, will you please welcome Liberty's own David Ring."

The applause was deafening, and there was no hesitancy on Ring's part this time. He popped right up from the seat beside me, carrying his notes in his right hand and approaching the podium with his signature walk. The clapping and cheering continued longer than usual, as if the crowd wanted to help him get there. Finally he did.

The noise eventually died down and Ring was center stage, just where he said he wanted to be. He fumbled for a moment with his notes, struggling to smooth out the creases from being folded and refolded in his pocket. He did so long enough that it no longer appeared his issue was about those pages—they just seemed to be something to channel his nervous energy into.

Finally he settled, gripping the wooden edges of the podium with both hands. He cleared his throat. But he didn't speak. My heart began racing faster than before, something I didn't think was possible. Was he choking up again?

He cleared his throat one more time, and a few random yells came from the crowd. "We love you, Ring!"

Then he opened his mouth and spoke his first words into a microphone, reverberating throughout the dead air. "I—I was—"

Suddenly he seemed overcome, as if those three syllables had drained him of all vocal strength. Ms. Myers suddenly stood up and walked to him, carrying a small glass of water with a straw sticking out of the top. She knew what he needed. He took it from her and sipped it, then set it down on the podium. She gave him a look of reassurance and walked back to her seat.

Just then, the sound of one of the metal doors creaking open broke the silence of the room. All eyes rotated to the right and landed on my dad. He slipped inside the door, but quickly realized he was now the center of attention. He looked across the gym at Ring and smiled—then gave him a thumbs-up.

Ring's demeanor instantly changed, as if that glass of water had quenched his soul. Suddenly. Strongly. He said, "Bo-un to woose. I was bo-un dead foh eighteen minutes. When I was bo-un, I was a stiwbo-un babeh. I was a dead babeh. I was a bwue babeh. They pu' my bodeh on a tabuh in the conuh and lef' meh foh dead."

An even deeper level of silence set in like fog over the entire gymnasium. I couldn't hear anyone breathing. There were no random coughs or sneezes. Nothing. This was Ring's time.

"Buh it's not ovuh until God say it's ovuh. When I was eweven yehs owd, my daddy got sick with cancuh of the wivuh. Two weeks afteh, my daddy died. I'm the babeh of eight and I'm not only the babeh of eight, I'm my momma's babeh boy. She did evwything fo' me. She fed me. She clothed me. She bathed me. She wauked wi' me and hewd me.

"Buh one day in my whife, when I was fouhteen yeuhs old, Momma got sick. The doctuh came tuh my famiwy an' said, 'Yo' momma whiw nevuh come home again. She has cancuh. She has six months, at the mos', to whiv.'

"I said, 'Not my momma! My momma whiw nevuh abandon me.' My momma towd me, 'I whiw nevuh weave you. I whiw nevuh abandon you.' I got down on my knees an' pwayed, 'God, don' take Momma! Don' take Momma! Don' take Momma!'

"Buh in Octobuh 1968, my momma took huh whast breath. And when my momma died, I didn't wan' to whiv. I wanted tuh die too."

Ring stopped and looked down at the podium for a moment. He wasn't talking about pain—he was living it out before us. I didn't turn around to look at the people in the bleachers, but I heard a few sniffles.

Ring took a deep breath and continued, "I didn't have one thing to whiv foh. Evwywheh I went, people made fun of me. They wooked at me and cawwed me evwy name othuh than my own. 'Wook, that boy walk funny! Wook, that boy talk funny!' I wen' home evwyday and got in bed, teuhs wolling down my face. Begging to die. I even twied to kiw mysewf. Evwybody gave up on meh.

"I gave up on meh."

Now the sniffles were becoming widespread. I looked over at my dad leaning against the wall. His face was wet, his astonishment clear as he focused on Ring.

"One night, I went to chuch. I didn't want to go to chuch. I'd been to chuch and I knew God dint wuv meh. If God wuv me, why God take 'way Momma? Why God pickin' on meh? God don' even whike meh.

"But that night, I foun' out one thing. I foun' out that God does wuv me—and has a wonduhful pwan foh my whife. I foun' out that I'm not okay, buh that's okay. God wuvs me jus' the way I am."

Now he was looking out on the audience, speaking with an authority we'd never have thought possible. "When I fuhst came to Wibuhty, I was a dead boy. I was a mean boy. An' some of yuh didn't know wha' to do with meh. Some of yuh made fun of meh, and that's okay. Buh yuh saw something change in meh. Today I wan' to tew yuh what it was. I'm not the same anymuh. I gave my whife to God. I don' want to die anymuh, I want to whiv! Why? Because I got something wuth whiving foh."

He looked at me, then over to Ms. Myers. A small grin broke out across his face as if he knew this moment was what he was made to do. "We thwo away bwoken things, buh God don't. God use bwoken things. God saw a dead babeh and God bwought that dead babeh to whife. And if I can whiv, I pwomise yuh can whiv too."

"I have cewebwal pawsy—what's yo' pwobwem?" His question lodged somewhere in my chest, and I couldn't quite swallow it. "Evwybody want to be wuved. Evwybody want to be wuved. God wuvs yuh. And Wing wuvs yuh too."

Then he walked away from that podium as if it were no more than a math problem he'd solved on the blackboard. He sat down beside me on the front row as a silent, stunned gymnasium sat behind us, still processing what they had just witnessed. The sniffles were now nearly universal.

Then, like the early sprinkles of rain, a few people began clapping. Then a few more.

And just like that, the deluge was released as the entire crowd stood to their feet, applauding wildly. Loud whistles rang out, and people began exchanging hugs. The emotion was too thick in the air to disperse on its own. Many were wiping their tears with their sleeves, and a number of football players turned away, seeming to have something in their eyes.

There was no formal dismissal. Eventually the crowd began to disperse to their weekend and their real lives. Still, a steady stream of people gathered around Ring, shaking his hand and hugging him. I heard snatches of other voices, people sharing their own stories with him and with each other.

Something was on the loose in that room. It was, you might say, a love mob.

And appropriately enough, he was the ringleader.

A bit reluctantly, I left Ring to his moment, sensing that these moments were delicate and couldn't be clung to. I joined my dad by the door. I might have said those four words, *I told you so*, but instead all I said was contained in a healthy man-hug. And his reply was eloquent in the ferocity of the smile on his face.

Then we stood there, leaning against the wall, watching Ring do something we now knew he was absolutely measured and outfitted to do, even with a weak, cerebral palsy–laden body. Particularly because of that body. Ring was inspiring, changing everyone around him, simply by being Ring.

I soaked it all in the best I could for a high school senior, knowing that this was not the ending of a journey for Ring. It was only the first step, stumbling but certain.

Epilogue

That May, wearing blue gowns and square caps, we each walked in front of our peers and families. Ring's journey across the small stage brought the entire audience immediately to its feet. Principal Davenport had given the usual instructions to hold all applause until the end, but with Ring that wasn't going to happen. Finally, the principal offered a smiling surrender. He motioned for the faculty sitting on the stage to join the ovation.

After our caps were thrown high, Ring celebrated with us and his family. Loretta was there, smiling as she stood quietly to the side. Debbie had found another man and had run off with him to live up north somewhere.

After high school, Tim went away to school and we eventually lost touch, as happens with early friendships. But Ring, Jeff, and I all attended college locally at William Jewell, living in the same dorm. College life was not always easy for Ring. He was lonely in the larger pool of people, where he didn't always enjoy the notoriety and acceptance he'd had in high school.

We didn't baby him, but we sure as heck didn't let him be mistreated. We were more friends than protectors, but being a protector is one of the most important parts of being a friend, cerebral palsy or not. And after a few months at college, Ring slowly began to endear himself to those around him, just as he always had done.

Like the rest of us, he dated a few girls during those days, but none of them ever became steady or serious. One girl named Opal finally won his heart—only to shatter it. So devastated was Ring that Dad and I felt it necessary to take him away to my grandparents' house for a few days. Again, with the determination he showed over and over, he got his life and emotions back on track. When the worst of it was over, we joked with him that it was all for the best—did he really want to be married to an Opal Ring?

Jeff and I pledged the Lambda Chi Alpha fraternity and got accepted. Once in, we used our status in the frat to advocate for other men to be accepted. Ring came on board with us. We'd gotten the band back together. Eventually, I would become president of the fraternity.

We watched with keen interest as Ring moved ever closer to his vision for his life. Doors began to open, even during college, for him to speak before audiences. A few notable evangelists, inspired by his story and his dream, brought him on as their "opening act." The two men who influenced him the most were Clyde Chiles and Jim McNiel. They took him under their wings, seeing his potential and feeling drawn to him in the same way my family was.

The boy whom no one believed could put together coherent sentences was now a budding professional speaker. I use the term "professional" only in the strictest sense of the word. He was still young and had much to learn. His payment may have been only a few dollars or a Shoney's platter, but he began to grow in his craft and calling—and people's hearts were moved by his story and spirit.

As college neared its conclusion, Ring applied to a Southern Baptist seminary. The day the letter came was a monumental moment in his life. It was a rejection letter. Polite, but a rejection nonetheless. Like poison served in a crystal goblet.

Some caring friends did a little digging and found the reason for the rejection: his disability. The powers that be at the seminary just didn't believe he could be an evangelist with his limitations. It was another blow in the boxing match that was his life. He lay bleeding on the proverbial mat for a few days, but got back up before the ten count. He always did.

He was true to what he had heard by the river years ago, on that night when God spoke to him. Ring took on every challenge with his eyes stubbornly fixed on where he wanted to go and who he wanted to serve. Nothing else mattered. What he believed, no one would have blamed him for doubting. The way he pursued it, nothing and nobody was going to get in the way. "Ring," I would say, "you are one stubborn individual." And he would just smile back, with that gleam in his eye that I'd seen ever since he told me he was going to speak at a school assembly.

In any fight there's a "knock-down moment," when you wonder if the blow was just too much to overcome, and the effort of getting off the canvas too much to summon. For Ring, a little slip of paper was that moment. It was the seminary telling him he couldn't do what God told him to do.

It's always that moment when the boxer gets up, against all odds, that you know he has what it takes to win. That's how it went with Ring's battle.

Speaking opportunities started opening up. More and more of them, from a trickle to a flood. Then, in June 1978, the main door swung wide open for him. He was invited to Atlanta to speak to the Southern Baptist Convention. He was only twenty-four years old, the youngest person to ever address the general conference. And it was this convention's seminary that had mailed him that rejection slip. The symbolism of that development wasn't lost on Ring.

Twenty-two thousand pastors and their wives heard him share his story that day. He had shared it many times by now, even when it seemed no one really wanted to listen.

They were listening now.

After that moment, he became a coveted speaker on a national stage, requested at more churches and events than he could possibly book. He also became close friends with a regular speaker on the *Old Time Gospel Hour* with Dr. Jerry Falwell, whose church and national television program brought Ring's story and personality to millions more listeners. Soon he was no longer a national speaker; he was an international one.

Meanwhile, his life was being enriched in other ways. In May 1979, Ring was speaking in St. Charles, Missouri—the same town where he'd suffered the worst grief of losing his mom and the worst of the bullying as well. It was there that he met a beautiful young woman named Karen.

Their connection was instant.

They began dating and soon it was apparent that, though Karen had dated strong, athletic boys in the past, Ring was her buried treasure. She wanted to spend the rest of her life exploring the spiritual and emotional riches she found in that treasure.

Oddly enough, it was not Karen's family who had a problem with the possibility of marriage. They wondered whether or not the two could have children, but ultimately they offered their full blessing. It was Ring's family, especially Loretta, who tried to sabotage the couple's joy. At one point they succeeded in talking him out of the marriage.

But Karen wouldn't give up on Ring or the life she knew they could have together. They were finally married two and a half years later.

Five weeks after the wedding, the Rings were busy with an appearance in Memphis when Karen began to experience morning sickness. A few weeks later, she called Ring on the road to tell him the news. She was pregnant—and with that, all questions and doubts about his ability to become a father were settled.

On June 21, 1982, April Jane was born into the world—a beautiful baby girl. Two more baby girls would follow, Ashley Dawn and Amy Joy, and one son, Nathan David. All four children were healthy and perfect. God had performed another miracle. Ring's worst fears, those of his condition being a legacy, were set to rest forever.

As for our friend Jeff, he had always been like a brother. But he made that official when he married my sister, Kathy. Ring recalls that the night of his conversion, April 17, 1970, Kathy gleefully told him, "Now we share a birthday." April 17 was the day she entered the world and the day he entered the kingdom. Each year they call each other on the phone to celebrate together.

As for me, I married my incredible wife, Jenna, after college. We have two beautiful children, Amanda and Mathew.

I became a teacher, then a school principal—and then submitted to the same calling my father had modeled for me all my life. For more than thirty years I've been a pastor, most recently in Coral Gables, Florida.

David Ring was in my wedding, I was in his, and we've been in each other's lives ever since. We talk frequently and marvel together over all the things that God has done since that day at the bus stop.

What I never realized was that there was a side to his story I had never known. When he visited our church in 2013, he finally opened this chapter of his life to me for the first time. It was a secret he had clutched tightly for forty-six years. As we sat together in a restaurant, I heard the truth about the sexual abuse that had been inflicted on my friend all those years ago. I'd had no suspicions that Ring's struggles could have gone to a deeper level even than his physical condition. I struggled to accept the horrible narrative he shared with me.

It was the beginning of one more incredible challenge for David Ring to take on. He felt that it was time for his family to know the truth. Even Karen had never been entrusted with this deeply buried secret. No one had, except one pastor and his wife, who gave Ring one of his first opportunities to speak many decades ago. Ring had revealed the abuse to them early in his college career, but didn't tell anyone else until 2013. After finally telling Karen, Ring went into counseling as he wrestled with the tragic realities of his past.

Once again, he simply wouldn't be beaten. As he had once climbed out of that pitch-black basement into the light of a new life and new relationships with the people around him and left that basement behind, now there was a sub-cellar—an even deeper darkness—that needed to finally be cleaned out and boarded up forever. The truth he fully understood was that it was all part of the message God wanted him to share. Just as there were people who needed the basic joy he had discovered, there were others with deeper sufferings, with secrets of their own, who needed to know the depths of God's grace.

I look back now and realize it all began in Liberty. That was the name of the town where our paths crossed in 1969—but it was also the name of the thing we all found in the story he lived out. I first met him in a dark basement, though he no longer remembers that day or that meeting. He chalks it up to the despair he felt then, the longing for death's release. But he does recall his liberty. He recalls being freed from darkness. From abuse. From hopelessness.

It's also fascinating to me that he has a vivid memory of a day he stumbled out of his house, wanting to create as much distance between himself and Debbie as possible. He remembers walking three blocks and wandering into our church as no more than a rest stop on his miserable jaunt.

He didn't know it, but this was Vacation Bible School time. A greeter asked him, "Are you here for VBS?" He had no idea what that was, but nodded.

The usher, he says, led him down the stairs into another basement. It couldn't have been a comfortable prospect, but Ring says that's when he first remembers meeting me. I would have been helping with children. He doesn't remember our first meeting in his basement, and I actually do not remember our first meeting in this one.

Two basements. One shadowed in the darkest secrets of shame and loss, the other filled with light and happy children; a picture of hope and a foreshadowing of friendship and new life.

Today, Ring possesses a new passion in an older body: to help bring healing to the millions around the world who have faced the same horrific realities of physical and sexual abuse that he faced. His mission may have refocused itself, but his message remains the same: "God don't thwo away bwoken things. God use bwoken things."

Writer's Note

When I set about the daunting task of penning the true story of David Ring's life, I was immediately confronted with both an obstacle and a mystery. In the end, those two disparate variables became the framework for this book.

The greatest obstacle to writing David's story was doing so from a first-person perspective, which was our original idea. He and I agreed that his limitations in verbal communication would make this approach difficult, and perhaps even less believable in terms of finding his narrative voice.

As we contemplated how to go about crafting the manuscript, I asked him a question regarding the aforesaid mystery: how did a suicidal teenage boy with cerebral palsy manage to randomly stumble into a church service filled with older people—and on a weeknight at that? This did not sound like any teenager I knew, and as a former public educator turned youth pastor for over fifteen years, I've known a few.

His response changed everything. He told me that when he was sixteen years old, the local pastor's son, also named

David, had unsuccessfully attempted to befriend him. Despite Ring's constant resistance to his kindness, David Wideman just wouldn't give up. That was why Ring was willing to go to church that night—Wideman had long been planting seeds of friendship that one day sprouted into a transformed life of redemption and purpose.

That piece of information changed everything. We approached Wideman (as we affectionately call him) about the idea of writing this story from his teenage perspective in the 1960s. He was more than gracious in lending us the use of his name and offering helpful details about his life, perspective, and family.

Writing from Wideman's perspective has allowed me to say things about Ring that he wouldn't say about himself—or even couldn't say about himself. Add to that the fact that David Wideman and David Ring are still good friends today, and Wideman became an incredible source for important details and ideas. Although he did not physically join us in the nitty-gritty of the writing process itself, his willingness to offer information and to let this incredible story be told within the dramatized context of his own adolescence created a unique paradigm for the narrative—one we are so very pleased with. For this we are forever indebted to Wideman and his family.

As far as the writing process goes, this book is a work of nonfiction with ribbons of fictitious elements running throughout. What I mean is that I let the basic facts of David Ring's life and story serve as a framework. Ring's family history. The town of Liberty. Ring's disabilities and hardships. Wideman's friendship and family dynamics. The life details of Ring's mother and father. The unthinkable abuses Ring suffered. His powerful transformation and the subsequent relationships God granted him in the community and school. The unlikely moment where he publicly shared his faith. All of these are actual occurrences written as accurately as possible.

But I want you to understand that around these facts, I took the "liberty" of adding other minor characters, changing names or dates to protect certain people, or adding events to help the story move along. All told, the best way to process this book is similar to watching a movie that is based on a true story such as *A Beautiful Mind*, *The Blind Side*, *Amazing Grace*, or *Remember the Titans*. Regardless, the infrastructure of this story is quite solid in its truth. My hope and prayer is that our expression of the narrative, even the fictionalized elements, will impact the way you look at life, faith, and friendship.

If they do, then you are yet another person touched by God's mercy and grace that continue to be the real life of David Ring.

John Driver

As a nationally known speaker since 1973, **David Ring** shares his story with over one hundred thousand people each year at churches, conventions, schools, and corporate events. He has been featured on numerous occasions on several nationally televised programs.

David and his wife, Karen, make their home in Nashville, Tennessee. They are the parents of four children, April, Ashley, Nathan, and Amy Joy. They are Poppy and Bella to two grandsons, Carter David and Cooper Solomon, and a granddaughter, Alexandra Jane.

John Driver is an educator turned pastor and ministry leader who created Ignition 7, a global initiative of videos, books, apps, and resources crafted to equip people to be sustained in their faith. He is the author or coauthor of more than a dozen books, including *Reggie: You Can't Change Your Past, but You Can Change Your Future* (with Reggie Dabbs) and the upcoming *Diary of a Jackwagon* (with comedian Tim Hawkins). He lives with his wife and daughter, Laura and Sadie, in Tennessee.

David Wideman has been a pastor at Christ Journey Church in Coral Gables, Florida, since 1983. As executive pastor for campus operations, he oversees the finances, facilities, and staffing for a multi-campus church reaching thousands on physical campuses and online. He and his wife, Jenna, have two adult children and live in Miami, Florida.

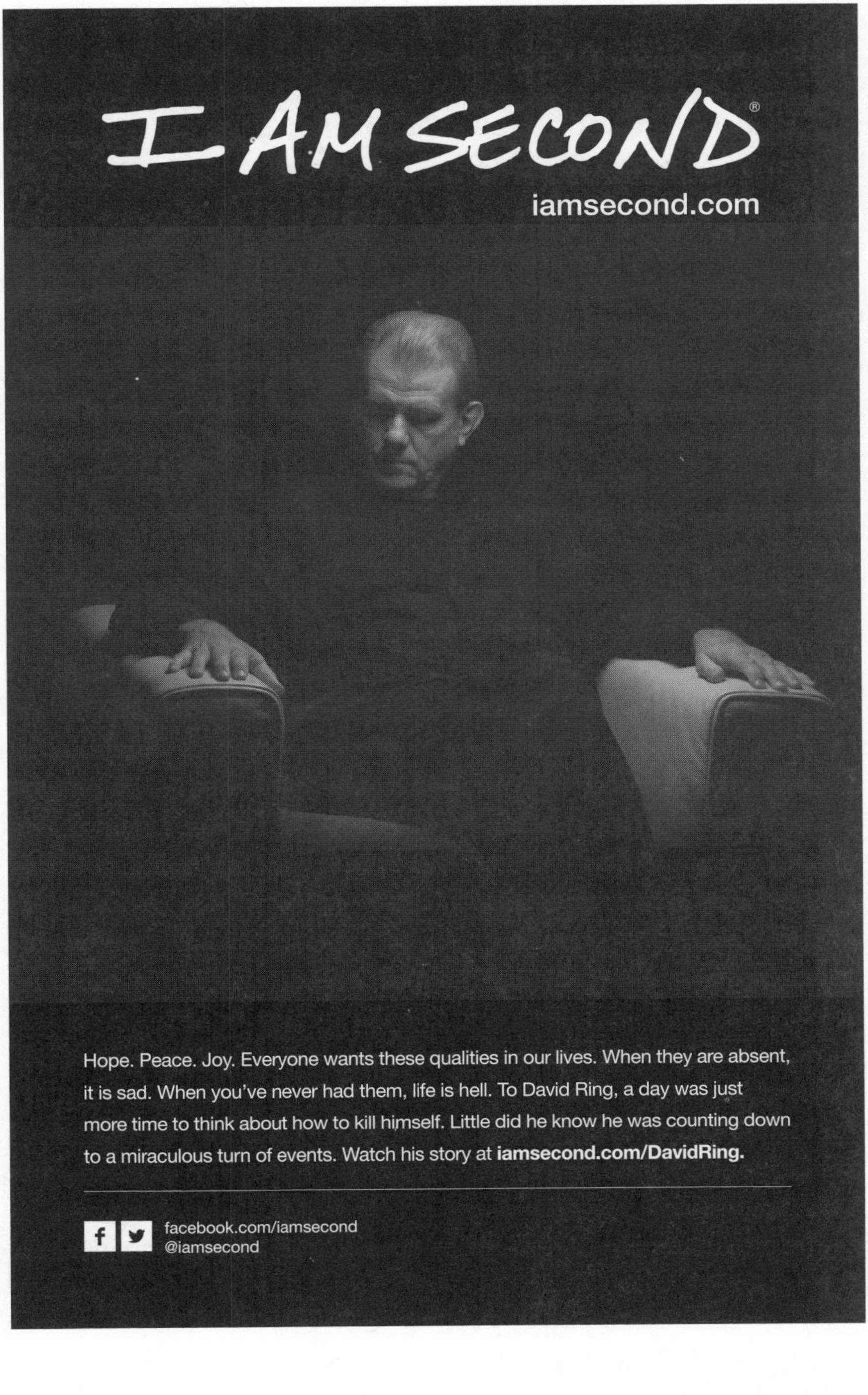
I AM SECOND®
iamsecond.com
Hope. Peace. Joy. Everyone wants these qualities in our lives. When they are absent, it is sad. When you've never had them, life is hell. To David Ring, a day was just more time to think about how to kill himself. Little did he know he was counting down to a miraculous turn of events. Watch his story at iamsecond.com/DavidRing.
facebook.com/iamsecond
@iamsecond